# The Modes of Ancient Greek Music

W0013554

D. B. Monro

**Alpha Editions**

This edition published in 2023

ISBN : 9789357913621

Design and Setting By
**Alpha Editions**
www.alphaedis.com
Email - info@alphaedis.com

# Contents

PREFACE............................................................- 1 -

§ 1. Introductory.................................................- 3 -

§ 2. Statement of the question.............................- 4 -

§ 3. The Authorities. ..........................................- 5 -

§ 4. The Early Poets. .........................................- 6 -

§ 5. Plato. ........................................................- 8 -

§ 6. Heraclides Ponticus....................................- 10 -

§ 7. Aristotle—the Politics.................................- 12 -

§ 8. The Aristotelian Problems. ..........................- 14 -

§ 9. The Rhetoric..............................................- 15 -

§ 10. Aristoxenus. .............................................- 16 -

§ 11. *Names of Keys* (hypo-)............................- 18 -

§ 12. Plutarch's Dialogue on Music. ...................- 19 -

§ 13. Modes employed on different Instruments. ...- 23 -

§ 14. Recapitulation— harmonia and tonos...........- 24 -

§ 15. The Systems of Greek Music.......................- 25 -

§ 16. The Standard Octachord System..................- 26 -

§ 17. Earlier Heptachord Scales...........................- 28 -

§ 18. The Perfect System. ..................................- 30 -

§ 19. Relation of System and Key. ......................- 34 -

§ 20. Tonality of the Greek musical scale..............- 36 -

§ 21. The Species of a Scale. .............................- 39 -

§ 22. The Scales as treated by Aristoxenus...........- 40 -

§ 23. The Seven Species. ...................................- 45 -

§ 24. Relation of the Species to the Keys. ............- 47 -

§ 25. The Ethos of Music...................................- 50 -

§ 26. The Ethos of the Genera and Species. ............................- 53 -

§ 27. The Musical Notation. ....................................- 54 -

§ 28. Traces of the Species in the Notation. ..........................- 60 -

§ 29. Ptolemy's Scheme of Modes. ...............................- 62 -

§ 30. Nomenclature by Position. ................................- 64 -

§ 31. Scales of the Lyre and Cithara. .............................- 66 -

§ 32. Remains of Greek Music. .................................- 69 -

§ 33. Modes of Aristides Quintilianus. ..........................- 74 -

§ 34. Credibility of Aristides Quintilianus...........................- 75 -

§ 35. Evidence for Scales of different species. ....................- 79 -

§ 36. Conclusion. ...........................................- 84 -

§ 37. Epilogue—Speech and Song.............................- 87 -

APPENDIX...............................................- 95 -

ef♯ gabc♯ de...............................................- 113 -

FOOTNOTES ...........................................- 114 -

# PREFACE

The present essay is the sequel of an article on Greek music which the author contributed to the new edition of *Smith's Dictionary of Greek and Roman Antiquities* (London, 1890-91, art. MUSICA). In that article the long-standing controversy regarding the nature of the ancient musical Modes was briefly noticed, and some reasons were given for dissenting from the views maintained by Westphal, and now very generally accepted. A full discussion of the subject would have taken up more space than was then at the author's disposal, and he accordingly proposed to the Delegates of the Clarendon Press to treat the question in a separate form. He has now to thank them for undertaking the publication of a work which is necessarily addressed to a very limited circle.

The progress of the work has been more than once delayed by the accession of materials. Much of it was written before the author had the opportunity of studying two very interesting documents first made known in the course of last year in the *Bulletin de correspondance hellénique* and the *Philologus*, viz. the [Pg x] so-called Seikelos inscription from Tralles, and a fragment of the *Orestes* of Euripides. But a much greater surprise was in store. The book was nearly ready for publication last November, when the newspapers reported that the French scholars engaged in excavating on the site of Delphi had found several pieces of musical notation, in particular a hymn to Apollo dating from the third century B.C. As the known remains of Greek music were either miserably brief, or so late as hardly to belong to classical antiquity, it was thought best to wait for the publication of the new material. The French School of Athens must be congratulated upon the good fortune which has attended their enterprise, and also upon the excellent form in which its results have been placed, within a comparatively short time, at the service of students. The writer of these pages, it will be readily understood, had especial reason to be interested in the announcement of a discovery which might give an entirely new complexion to the whole argument. It will be for the reader to determine whether the main thesis of the book has gained or lost by the new evidence.

Mr. Hubert Parry prefaces his suggestive treatment of Greek music by some remarks on the difficulty of the subject. 'It still seems possible,' he observes, 'that a large portion of what has passed into the domain of "well-authenticated fact" is complete misapprehension, as Greek scholars have not time for a thorough study of music up to the standard required to judge securely of the matters in question, and [Pg xi] musicians as a rule are not extremely intimate with Greek' (*The Art of Music*, p. 24). To the present writer, who has no claim to the title of musician, the scepticism expressed in these words appears to be well founded. If his interpretation of the ancient texts furnishes musicians like Mr. Parry with a somewhat more trustworthy basis for their criticism of Greek music as an art, his object will be fully attained.

# § 1. Introductory.

The modes of ancient Greek music are of interest to us, not only as the forms under which the Fine Art of Music was developed by a people of extraordinary artistic capability, but also on account of the peculiar ethical influence ascribed to them by the greatest ancient philosophers. It appears from a well-known passage in the *Republic* of Plato, as well as from many other references, that in ancient Greece there were certain kinds or forms of music, which were known by national or tribal names—Dorian, Ionian, Phrygian, Lydian and the like: that each of these was believed to be capable, not only of expressing particular emotions, but of reacting on the sensibility in such a way as to exercise a powerful and specific influence in the formation of character: and consequently that the choice, among these varieties, of the musical forms to be admitted into the education of the state, was a matter of the most serious practical concern. If on a question of this kind we are inclined to distrust the imaginative temper of Plato we have only to turn to the discussion of the same subject in the *Politics* of Aristotle, and we shall find the Platonic view criticised in some important details, but treated in the main as being beyond controversy.

The word **harmonia**, 'harmony,' applied to these forms of music by Plato and Aristotle, means literally 'fitting' or 'adjustment,' hence the 'tuning' of a series of notes on any principle, the formation of a 'scale' or 'gamut.' Other ancient writers use the word **tropos**, whence the Latin *modus* and our mood or 'mode,' generally employed in this sense by English scholars. The word 'mode' is open to the objection that in modern music it has a meaning which assumes just what it is our present business to prove or disprove about the 'modes' of Greek music. The word 'harmony,' however, is still more misleading, and on the whole it seems best to abide by the established use of 'mode' as a translation of **harmonia**, trusting that the context will show when the word has its distinctively modern sense, and when it simply denotes a musical scale of some particular kind.

The rhythm of music is also recognized by both Plato and Aristotle as an important element in its moral value. On this part of the subject, however, we have much less material for a judgement. Plato goes on to the rhythms after he has done with the modes, and lays down the principle that they must not be complex or varied, but must be the rhythms of a sober and brave life. But he confesses that he cannot tell which these are (**poia de poiou biou mimêmata ouk echô legein**), and leaves the matter for future inquiry [1].

# § 2. Statement of the question.

What then are the musical forms to which Plato and Aristotle ascribe this remarkable efficacy? And what is the source of their influence on human emotion and character?

There are two obvious relations in which the scales employed in any system of music may stand to each other. They may be related as two keys of the same mode in modern music: that is to say, we may have to do with a scale consisting of a fixed succession of intervals, which may vary in pitch—may be 'transposed,' as we say, from one pitch or key to another. Or the scales may differ as the Major mode differs from the Minor, namely in the order in which the intervals follow each other. In modern music we have these two modes, and each of them may be in any one of twelve keys. It is evidently possible, also, that a name such as Dorian or Lydian might denote a particular mode taken in a particular key—that the scale so called should possess a definite pitch as well as a definite series of intervals.

According to the theory which appears now to prevail among students of Greek music, these famous names had a double application. There was a Dorian mode as well as a Dorian key, a Phrygian mode and a Phrygian key, and so on. This is the view set forth by Boeckh in the treatise which may be said to have laid the foundations of our knowledge of Greek music (*De Metris Pindari*, lib. III. cc. vii-xii). It is expounded, along with much subsidiary speculation, in the successive volumes which we owe to the fertile pen of Westphal; and it has been adopted in the learned and excellent *Histoire et Théorie de la Musique de l'Antiquité* of M. Gevaert. According to these high authorities the Greeks had a system of key (**tonoi**), and also a system of modes (**harmoniai**), the former being based solely upon difference of pitch, the latter upon the 'form' or species (**eidos**) of the octave scale, that is to say, upon the order of the intervals which compose it.

---

# § 3. The Authorities.

The sources of our knowledge are the various systematic treatises upon music which have come down to us from Greek antiquity, together with incidental references in other authors, chiefly poets and philosophers. Of the systematic or 'technical' writers the earliest and most important is Aristoxenus, a pupil of Aristotle. His treatise on *Harmonics* (**harmonikê**) has reached us in a fragmentary condition, but may be supplemented to some extent from later works of the same school. Among the incidental notices of music the most considerable are the passages in the *Republic* and the *Politics* already referred to. To these we have to add a few other references in Plato and Aristotle; a long fragment from the Platonic philosopher Heraclides Ponticus, containing some interesting quotations from earlier poets; a number of detached observations collected in the nineteenth section of the Aristotelian *Problems*; and one or two notices preserved in lexicographical works, such as the *Onomasticon* of Pollux.

In these groups of authorities the scholars above mentioned find the double use which they believe to have been made of the names Dorian, Phrygian, Lydian and the rest. In Aristoxenus they recognise that these names are applied to a series of keys (**tonoi**), which differed in pitch only. In Plato and Aristotle they find the same names applied to scales called **harmoniai**, and these scales, they maintain, differed primarily in the order of their intervals. I shall endeavour to show that there was no such double use: that in the earlier periods of Greek music the scales in use, whether called **tonoi** or **harmoniai**, differed primarily in *pitch*: that the statements of ancient authors about them, down to and including Aristoxenus, agree as closely as there is reason to expect: and that the passages on which the opposite view is based—all of them drawn from comparatively late writers—either do not relate to these ancient scales at all, or point to the emergence in post-classical times of some new forms or tendencies of musical art. I propose in any case to adhere as closely as possible to a chronological treatment of the evidence which is at our command, and I hope to make it probable that the difficulties of the question may be best dealt with on this method.

# § 4. The Early Poets.

The earliest of the passages now in question comes from the poet Pratinas, a contemporary of Aeschylus. It is quoted by Heraclides Ponticus, in the course of a long fragment preserved by Athenaeus (xiv. cc. 19-21, p. 624 *c*-626 *a*). The words are:

mête syntonon diôke mête tan aneimenan
Iasti mousan, alla tan messan neôn
arouran aiolize tô melei.

'Follow neither a highly-strung music nor the low-pitched Ionian, but turning over the middle plough-land be an Aeolian in your melody.' Westphal takes the word **'Iasti** with **syntonon** as well as with **aneimenan**, and infers that there were two kinds of Ionian, a 'highly-strung' and a 'relaxed' or low-pitched. But this is not required by the words, and seems less natural than the interpretation which I have given. All that the passage proves is that in the time of Pratinas a composer had the choice of at least three scales: one (or more) of which the pitch was high (**syntonos**); another of low pitch (**aneimenê**), which was called *Ionian*; and a third, intermediate between the others, and known as *Aeolian*. Later in the same passage we are told that Pratinas spoke of the 'Aeolian harmony' (**prepei toi pasin aoidolabraktais Aiolis harmonia**). And the term is also found, with the epithet 'deep-sounding,' in a passage quoted from the hymn to Demeter of a contemporary poet, Lasus of Hermione (Athen. xiv. 624 *e*):

Damatra melpô Koran te Klymenoio alochon Meliboian,
hymnôn anagôn Aiolid' hama barybromon harmonian.

With regard to the Phrygian and Lydian scales Heraclides (*l. c.*) quotes an interesting passage from Telestes of Selinus, in which their introduction is ascribed to the colony that was said to have followed Pelops from Asia Minor to the Peloponnesus:

prôtoi para kratêras Hellênôn en aulois
synopadoi Pelopos matros oreias phrygion aeison nomon;
toi d' oxyphônois pêktidôn psalmois krekon
Dydion hymnon.

'The comrades of Pelops were the first who beside the Grecian cups sang with the flute (**aulos**) the Phrygian measure of the Great Mother; and these again by shrill-voiced notes of the *pectis* sounded a Lydian hymn.' The epithet **oxyphônos** is worth notice in connexion with other evidence of the high pitch of the music known as Lydian.  The Lydian mode is mentioned by Pindar, *Nem.* 4. 45:

**exyphaine glykeia kai tod' autika phorminx
Lydia syn harmonia melos pephilêmenon.**

The Dorian is the subject of an elaborate jest made at the expense of Cleon in the *Knights* of Aristophanes, ll. 985-996:

**alla kai tod' egô ge thaumazô tês hyomousias
autou phasi gar auton hoi paides hoi xynephoitôn
tên Dôristi monên enarmottesthai thama tên lyran,
allên d' ouk ethelein labein; kata ton kitharistên
orgisthent' apagein keleuein, hôs harmonian ho pais
outos ou dynatai mathein ên mê Dôrodokêsti.**

# § 5. Plato.

Following the order of time, we come next to the passage in the *Republic* (p. 398), where Socrates is endeavouring to determine the kinds of music to be admitted for the use of his future 'guardians,' in accordance with the general principles which are to govern their education. First among these principles is the condemnation of all undue expression of grief. 'What modes of music (**harmoniai**),' he asks, are plaintive (**thrênôdeis**)?' 'The *Mixo-lydian*,' Glaucon replies, 'and the *Syntono-lydian*, and such-like.' These accordingly Socrates excludes. 'But again, drunkenness and slothfulness are no less forbidden to the guardians; which of the modes are soft and convivial (**malakai te kai sympotikai**)?' '*Ionian*,' says Glaucon, 'and *Lydian*, those which are called slack (**chalarai**).' 'Which then remain?' 'Seemingly *Dorian* and *Phrygian*.' 'I do not know the modes,' says Socrates, 'but leave me one that will imitate the tones and accents of a brave man enduring danger or distress, fighting with constancy against fortune: and also one fitted for the work of peace, for prayer heard by the gods, for the successful persuasion or exhortation of men, and generally for the sober enjoyment of ease and prosperity.' Two such modes, one for Courage and one for Temperance, are declared by Glaucon to be found in the Dorian and the Phrygian. In the *Laches* (p. 188) there is a passing reference in which a similar view is expressed. Plato is speaking of the character of a brave man as being metaphorically a 'harmony,' by which his life is made consonant to reason—'a Dorian harmony,' he adds—playing upon the musical sense of the word—'not an Ionian, certainly not a Phrygian or a Lydian, but that one which only is truly Hellenic' (**atechnôs Dôristi, all' ouk Iasti, oiomai de oude Phrygisti oude Lydisti, all' hê per monê Hellênikê estin harmonia**). The exclusion of Phrygian may be due to the fact that the virtue discussed in the *Laches* is courage; but it is in agreement with Aristotle's opinion. The absence of Aeolian from both the Platonic passages seems to show that it had gone out of use in his time (but cp. p. 11).

The point of view from which Plato professes to determine the right modes to be used in his ideal education appears clearly in the passage of the *Republic*. The modes first rejected are those which are high in pitch. The Syntono-lydian or 'high-strung Lydian' is shown by its name to be of this class. The Mixo-lydian is similar, as we shall see from Aristotle and other writers. The second group which he condemns is that of the 'slack' or low-pitched. Thus it is on the profoundly Hellenic principle of choosing the mean between opposite extremes that he approves of the Dorian and Phrygian pitch. The application of this principle was not a new one, for it had been already laid down by Pratinas: **mête syntonon diôke mête tan aneimenan**.

The three chapters which Aristotle devotes to a discussion of the use of music in the state (*Politics* viii. cc. 5-7), and in which he reviews and criticises the Platonic treatment of the same subject, will be found entirely to bear out the view now taken. It is also supported by the commentary of Plutarch, in his dialogue on Music (cc. 15-17), of which we shall have something to say hereafter. Meanwhile, following the chronological order of our authorities, we come next to the fragment of Heraclides Ponticus already mentioned (Athen. xiv. p. 624 *c*-626 *a*).

---

# § 6. Heraclides Ponticus.

The chief doctrine maintained by Heraclides Ponticus is that there are three modes (**harmoniai**), belonging to the three Greek races—Dorian, Aeolian, Ionian. The Phrygian and Lydian, in his view, had no right to the name of mode or 'harmony' (**oud' harmonian phêsi dein kaleisthai tên Phrygion, kathaper oude tên Lydion**). The three which he recognized had each a marked ethos. The Dorian reflected the military traditions and temper of Sparta. The Aeolian, which Heraclides identified with the Hypo-dorian of his own time, answered to the national character of the Thessalians, which was bold and gay, somewhat overweening and self-indulgent, but hospitable and chivalrous. Some said that it was called Hypo-dorian because it was below the Dorian on the **aulos** or flute; but Heraclides thinks that the name merely expressed likeness to the Dorian character (**Dôrion men autên ou nomizein, prosempherê de pôs ekeinê**). The Ionian, again, was harsh and severe, expressive of the unkindly disposition fostered amid the pride and material welfare of Miletus. Heraclides is inclined to say that it was not properly a distinct musical scale or 'harmony,' but a strange aberration in the form of the musical scale (**tropon de tina thaumaston schêmatos harmonias**). He goes on to protest against those who do not appreciate differences of kind (**tas kat' eidos diaphoras**), and are guided only by the high or low pitch of the notes (**tê tôn phthongôn exytêti kai barytêti**); so that they make a Hyper-mixolydian, and another again above that. 'I do not see,' he adds, 'that the Hyper-phrygian has a distinct ethos; and yet some say that they have discovered a new mode (**harmonia**), the Hypo-phrygian. But a mode ought to have a distinct moral or emotional character (**eidos echein ethous hê pathous**), as the Locrian, which was in use in the time of Simonides and Pindar, but went out of fashion again.' The Phrygian and Lydian, as we have seen, were said to have been brought to the Peloponnesus by the followers of Pelops.

The tone as well as the substance of this extract makes it evident that the opinions of Heraclides on questions of theoretical music must be accepted with considerable reserve. The notion that the Phrygian and Lydian scales were 'barbarous' and opposed to Hellenic ethos was apparently common enough, though largely due (as we may gather from several indications) to national prejudice. But no one, except Heraclides, goes so far as to deny them the name of **harmonia**. The threefold division into Dorian, Aeolian and Ionian must also be arbitrary. It is to be observed that Heraclides obtains his Aeolian by identifying the Aeolian of Pratinas and other early poets with the mode called Hypo-dorian in his own time. The circumstance that Plato mentions neither Aeolian nor Hypo-dorian suggests rather that Aeolian had gone out of use before Hypo-dorian came in. The conjecture of Boeckh that

Ionian was the same as the later Hypo-phrygian (*De Metr. Pind.* iii. 8) is open to a similar objection. The Ionian mode was at least as old as Pratinas, whereas the Hypo-phrygian was a novelty in the time of Heraclides. The protest which Heraclides makes against classifying modes merely according to their pitch is chiefly valuable as proving that the modes were as a matter of fact usually classified from that point of view. It is far from proving that there was any other principle which Heraclides wished to adopt—such, for example, as difference in the intervals employed, or in their succession. His 'differences of kind' (**tas kat' eidos diaphoras**) are not necessarily to be explained from the technical use of **eidos** for the 'species' of the octave. What he complains of seems to be the multiplication of modes—Hyper-mixolydian, Hyper-phrygian, Hypo-phrygian—beyond the legitimate requirements of the art. The Mixo-lydian (*e.g.*) is high-pitched and plaintive: what more can the Hyper-mixolydian be? The Hypo-phrygian is a new mode: Heraclides denies it a distinctive ethos. His view seems to be that the number of modes should not be greater than the number of varieties in temper or emotion of which music is capable. But there is nothing to show that he did not regard pitch as the chief element, or one of the chief elements, of musical expression.

The absence of the name Hypo-lydian, taken with the description of Hypo-dorian as 'below the Dorian,' would indicate that the Hypo-dorian of Heraclides was not the later mode of that name, but was a semitone below the Dorian, in the place afterwards occupied by the Hypo-lydian. This is confirmed, as we shall see, by Aristoxenus (p. 18).

---

# § 7. Aristotle—the Politics.

Of the writers who deal with music from the point of view of the cultivated layman, Aristotle is undoubtedly the most instructive. The chapters in his *Politics* which treat of music in its relation to the state and to morality go much more deeply than Plato does into the grounds of the influence which musical forms exert upon temper and feeling. Moreover, Aristotle's scope is wider, not being confined to the education of the young; and his treatment is evidently a more faithful reflexion of the ordinary Greek notions and sentiment. He begins (*Pol.* viii. 5, p. 1340 *a* 38) by agreeing with Plato as to the great importance of the subject for practical politics. Musical forms, he holds, are not mere *symbols* (**sêmeia**), acting through association, but are an actual *copy* or reflex of the forms of moral temper (**en de tois melesin autois esti mimêmata tôn êthôn**); and this is the ground of the different moral influence exercised by different modes (**harmoniai**). By some of them, especially by the Mixo-lydian, we are moved to a plaintive and depressed temper (**diatithesthai odyrtikôterôs kai synestêkotôs mallon**); by others, such as those which are called the 'relaxed' (**aneimenai**), we are disposed to 'softness' of mind (**malakôterôs tên dianoian**). The Dorian, again, is the only one under whose influence men are in a middle and settled mood (**mesôs kai kathestêkotôs malista**): while the Phrygian makes them excited (**enthousiastikous**). In a later chapter (Pol. viii. 7, p. 1342 *a* 32), he returns to the subject of the Phrygian. Socrates, he thinks, ought not to have left it with the Dorian, especially since he condemned the flute (**aulos**), which has the same character among instruments as the Phrygian among modes, both being orgiastic and emotional. The Dorian, as all agree, is the most steadfast (**stasimôtatê**), and has most of the ethos of courage; and, as compared with other modes, it has the character which Aristotle himself regards as the universal criterion of excellence, viz. that of being the mean between opposite excesses. Aristotle, therefore, certainly understood Plato to have approved the Dorian and the Phrygian as representing the mean in respect of pitch, while other modes were either too high or too low. He goes on to defend the use of the 'relaxed' modes on the ground that they furnish a music that is still within the powers of those whose voice has failed from age, and who therefore are not able to sing the high-pitched modes (**oion tois apeirêkosi dia chronon ou rhadion adein tas syntonous harmonias, alla tas aneimenas hê physis hypoballei tois têlikoutois**). In this passage the meaning of the words **syntonos** and **aneimenos** is especially clear.

In the same discussion (c. 6), Aristotle refers to the distinction between music that is ethical, music suited to action, and music that inspires religious excitement (**ta men êthika, ta de praktika, ta ho enthousiastika**). The last of these kinds serves as a 'purification' (**katharsis**). The excitement is calmed by giving it vent; and the morbid condition of the ethos is met by music of high pitch and exceptional 'colour' (**tôn harmoniôn parekbaseis kai tôn melôn ta syntona kai parakechrôsmena**).

In a different connexion (*Pol.* iv. 3, p. 1290 *a* 20), dealing with the opinion that all forms of government are ultimately reducible to two, viz. oligarchy and democracy, Aristotle compares the view of some who held that there are properly only two musical modes, Dorian and Phrygian,—the other scales being mere varieties of these two. Rather, he says, there is in each case a right form, or two right forms at most, from which the rest are declensions (**parekbaseis**),—on one side to 'high-pitched' and imperious oligarchies, on the other to 'relaxed' and 'soft' forms of popular government (**oligarchikas men tas syntonôteras kai despotikônteras, tas d' aneimenas kai malakas dêmotikas**). This is obviously the Platonic doctrine of two right keys, holding the mean between high and low.

---

# § 8. The Aristotelian Problems.

Some further notices of the **harmoniai** or modes are contained in the so-called *Problems*,—a collection which is probably not the work of Aristotle himself, but can hardly be later than the Aristotelian age. What is said in it of the modes is clearly of the period before the reform of Aristoxenus. In one place (*Probl.* xix. 48) the question is asked why the Hypo-dorian and Hypo-phrygian are not used in the *chorus* of tragedy. One answer is that the Hypo-phrygian has the ethos of action (**êthos echei praktikon**), and that the Hypo-dorian is the expression of a lofty and unshaken character; both of these things being proper to the heroic personages on the stage, but not to the chorus, which represents the average spectator, and takes no part in the action. Hence the music suited to the chorus is that of emotion venting itself in passive complaint:—a description which fits the other modes, but least of all the exciting and orgiastic Hypo-phrygian. On the contrary (the writer adds) the passive attitude is especially expressed by the Mixo-lydian. The view here taken of the Hypo-dorian evidently agrees with that of Heraclides Ponticus (*supra*, p. 10).

The relation which Plato assumes between high pitch and the excitement of passion, and again between lowness of pitch and 'softness' or self-indulgence (**malakia kai argia**), is recognized in the *Problems*, xix. 49 **epei de ho men barys phthongos malakos kai êremaios estin, ho de oxys kinêtikos, k.t.l.**: 'since a deep note is soft and calm, and a high note is exciting, &c.'

# § 9. The Rhetoric.

The word **tonos** occurs several times in Aristotle with the sense of 'pitch,' but is not applied by him to the keys of music. The nearest approach to such a use may be found in a passage of the *Rhetoric* (iii. 1, p. 1403 *b* 27).

Speaking of the rise of acting (**hypokrisis**), which was originally the business of the poet himself, but had grown into a distinct art, capable of theoretical as well as practical treatment, he observes that a similar art might be formed for oratory. 'Such an art would lay down rules directing how to use the voice so as to suit each variety of feeling,—when it should be loud, when low, when intermediate;—and how to use the keys, when the pitch of the voice should be high or low or middle (**kai pôs tois tonois, oion oxeia kai bareia kai mesê**, sc. **phônê**); and the rhythms, which to use for each case. For there are three things which men study, viz. quantity (*i. e.* loudness of sound), tune, and rhythm (**tria gar esti peri hôn skopousi, tauta d' esti megethos, harmonia, rhythmos**).' The passage is interesting as showing the value which Aristotle set upon pitch as an element of effect. And the use of **harmonia** in reference to the pitch of the voice, and as virtually equivalent to **tonos**, is especially worthy of note.

# § 10. Aristoxenus.

Our next source of information is the technical writer Aristoxenus, a contemporary and pupil of Aristotle. Of his many works on the subject of music three books only have survived, bearing the title **harmonika otoicheia** [2]. In the treatment adopted by Aristoxenus the chapter on keys follows the chapter on 'systems' (**systêmata**). By a **systêma** he means a scale consisting of a certain succession of intervals: in other words, a series of notes whose relative pitch is determined. Such a system may vary in absolute pitch, and the **tonoi** or keys are simply the different degrees of pitch at which a particular system is taken (**tous tonous eph' ôn tithemena ta systêmata melôdeitai**). When the system and the key are both given it is evident that the whole series of notes is determined.

Aristoxenus is the chief authority on the keys of Greek music. In this department he is considered to have done for Greece what Bach's *Wohltemperirtes Clavier* did for modern Europe. It is true that the scheme of keys which later writers ascribe to him.

'No one,' says Aristoxenus (p. 37 Meib.), 'has told us a word about the keys, either how they are to be arrived at (**tina tropon lêpteon**), or from what point of view their number is to be determined. Musicians assign the place of the keys very much as the different cities regulate the days of the month. The Corinthians, for example, will be found counting a day as the tenth of the month, while with the Athenians it is the fifth, and in some other place the eighth. Some authorities on music (**harmonikoi**) say that the Hypo-dorian is the lowest key, the Mixo-lydian a semitone higher, the Dorian again a semitone higher, the Phrygian a tone above the Dorian, and similarly the Lydian a tone above the Phrygian. Others add the Hypo-phrygian flute [*i. e.* the scale of the flute so called] at the lower end of the list. Others, again, looking to the holes of the flute (**pros tên tôn aulôn trupêsin blepontes**), separate the three lowest keys, viz. the Hypo-phrygian, Hypo-dorian, and Dorian, by the interval of three-quarters of a tone (**trisi diesesin**), but the Phrygian from the Dorian by a tone, the Lydian from the Phrygian again by three-quarters of a tone, and the Mixo-lydian from the Lydian by a like interval. But as to what determines the interval between one key and another they have told us nothing.'

It will be seen that (with one marked exception) there was agreement about the order of the keys in respect of pitch, and that some at least had reduced the intervals to the succession of tones and semitones which characterises the diatonic scale. The exception is the Mixo-lydian, which some ranked immediately below the Dorian, others above the Lydian. Westphal attributes this strange discrepancy to the accidental displacing of some words in the MSS. of Aristoxenus [3]. However this may be, it is plain that in the time of Aristoxenus considerable progress had been made towards the scheme of keys which was afterwards connected with his name. This may be represented by the following table, in which for the sake of comparison the later Hypo-lydian and Hypo-dorian are added in brackets:

Mixo-lydian
semitone - {
Lydian
tone -{
Phrygian
tone -{
Dorian
semitone - {
Hypo-dorian   [Hypo-lydian]
tone -{
Hypo-phrygian
tone -{
[Hypo-dorian]

# § 11. *Names of Keys* (hypo-).

A point that deserves special notice at this place is the use of the prefix *Hypo-* (**hypo-**) in the names of keys. In the final Aristoxenean system *Hypo-* implies that a key is lower by the interval of a Fourth than the key to whose name it is prefixed. This convention served to bring out the special relation between the two keys, viz. to show that they are related (to use modern language) as the keys of a tonic and dominant. In the scheme of keys now in question there is only one instance of this use of *Hypo-*, namely in the Hypo-phrygian, the most recently introduced. It must have been on the analogy of this name that the term Hypo-dorian was shifted from the key immediately below the Dorian to the new key a Fourth below it, and that the new term Hypo-lydian was given to the old Hypo-dorian in accordance with its similar relation to the Lydian. In the time of Aristoxenus, then, this technical sense of *Hypo-* had not yet been established, but was coming into use. It led naturally to the employment of *Hyper-* in the inverse sense, viz. to denote a key a Fourth higher (the key of the sub-dominant). By further steps, of which there is no record, the Greek musicians arrived at the idea of a key for every semitone in the octave; and thus was formed the system of thirteen keys, ascribed to Aristoxenus by later writers. (See the scheme at the end of this book, Table II.) Whether in fact it was entirely his work may be doubted. In any case he had formed a clear conception—the want of which he noted in his predecessors—of the principles on which a theoretically complete scheme of keys should be constructed.

In the discussions to which we have been referring, Aristoxenus invariably employs the word **tonos** in the sense of 'key.' The word **harmonia** in his writings is equivalent to 'Enharmonic genus' (**genos enarmonion**), the *genus* of music which made use of the Enharmonic *diësis* or quarter-tone. Thus he never speaks, as Plato and Aristotle do, of the Dorian (or Phrygian or Lydian) **harmonia**, but only of the **tonoi** so named. There is indeed one passage in which certain octave scales are said by Aristoxenus to have been called **harmoniai**: but this, as will be shown, is a use which is to be otherwise explained (see p. 54).

# § 12. Plutarch's Dialogue on Music.

After the time of Aristoxenus the technical writers on music make little or no use of the term **harmonia**. Their word for 'key' is **tonos**; and the octachord scales which are distinguished by the succession of their intervals are called 'species of the octave' (**eidê tou dia pasôn**). The modes of the classical period, however, were still objects of antiquarian and philosophic interest, and authors who treated them from this point of view naturally kept up the old designation. A good specimen of the writings of this class has survived in the *dialogus de musicâ* of Plutarch. Like most productions of the time, it is mainly a compilation from earlier works now lost. Much of it comes from Aristoxenus, and there is therefore a special fitness in dealing with it in this place, by way of supplement to the arguments drawn directly from the Aristoxenean *Harmonics*. The following are the chief passages bearing on the subject of our enquiry:

(1) In cc. 15-17 we find a commentary of some interest on the Platonic treatment of the modes. Plutarch is dwelling on the superiority of the older and simpler music, and appeals to the opinion of Plato.

'The Lydian mode (**harmonia**) Plato objects to because it is high (**oxeia**) and suited to lamentation. Indeed it is said to have been originally devised for that purpose: for Aristoxenus tells us, in his first book on Music, that Olympus first employed the Lydian mode on the flute in a dirge (**epikêdeion aulêsai Lydisti**) over the Python. But some say that Melanippides began this kind of music. And Pindar in his paeans says that the Lydian mode (**harmonia**) was first brought in by Anthippus in an ode on the marriage of Niobe. But others say that Torrhebus first used that mode, as Dionysius the Iambus relates.'

'The Mixo-lydian, too, is pathetic and suitable to tragedy. And Aristoxenus says that Sappho was the inventor of the Mixo-lydian, and that from her the tragic poets learned it. They combined it with the Dorian, since that mode gives grandeur and dignity, and the other pathos, and these are the two elements of tragedy. But in his Historical Treatise on Music (**historika tês harmonias hypomnêmata**) he says that Pythoclides the flute-player was the discoverer of it. And Lysis says that Lamprocles the Athenian, perceiving that in it the disjunctive tone (**diazeuxis**) is not where it was generally supposed to be, but is at the upper end of the scale, made the form of it to be that of the octave from Paramesê to Hypatê Hypatôn (**toiouton autês apergasasthai to schêma hoion to apo paramesês epi hypatên hypatôn**). Moreover, it is said that the relaxed Lydian (**epaneimenên Lydisti**), which is the opposite of the Mixo-lydian, being similar to the Ionian (**paraplêsian ousan tê Iadi**), was invented by Damon the Athenian.'

'These modes then, the one plaintive, the other relaxed (**eklelymenê**), Plato properly rejected, and chose the Dorian, as befitting warlike and temperate men.'

In this passage the 'high-pitched Lydian' (**Syntonolydisti**) of Plato is called simply Lydian. There is every reason to suppose that it is the mode called Lydian by Aristotle and Heraclides Ponticus [4]. If this is so, it follows almost of necessity that the Lydian of Plato, called slack (**chalara**) by him—Plutarch's **epaneimenê Lydisti**—is to be identified with the later

Hypo-lydian. The point, however, is not free from difficulty: for (as we have seen, p. 18), the name Hypo-lydian is not in the list of keys given by Aristoxenus—the key which was ultimately called Hypo-lydian being known to him as the Hypo-dorian. If, however, the confusion in the nomenclature of the keys was as great as Aristoxenus himself describes, such a contradiction as this cannot be taken to prove much. [5]

The statement that the 'relaxed Lydian' was the opposite of the Mixo-lydian, and similar to the Ionian, has given rise to much speculation. In what sense, we naturally ask, can a key or a mode be said to be 'opposite' or 'similar' to another? I venture to think that it is evidently a mere paraphrase of Plato's language. The relaxed Lydian is opposed to the Mixo-lydian because it is at the other end of the scale in pitch; and it is similar to the Ionian because the two are classed together (as **chalarai**) by Plato.

The Mixo-lydian, according to Aristoxenus, was employed by the tragic poets in close union with the Dorian mode (**labontas syzeuxai tê Dôristi**). The fact that the Mixo-lydian was just a Fourth higher than the Dorian must have made the transition from the one to the other a natural and melodious one. As Aristoxenus suggested, it would be especially used to mark the passage from grandeur and dignity to pathos which is the chief characteristic of tragedy (**hê men to**

**megaloprepes kai axiômatikon apodidôsin, hê de to pathêtikon, memiktai de dia toutôn tragôdia**). It is worth noticing that this relation obtained in the scheme of the musicians who did not arrange the keys according to the diatonic scale, but in some way suggested by the form of the flute (**hoi pros tên tôn aulôn trypêsin blepontes**). It may therefore be supposed to have been established before the relative pitch of other keys had been settled.

So far the passage of Plutarch goes to confirm the view of the Platonic modes according to which they were distinguished chiefly, if not wholly, by difference of pitch. We come now, however, to a statement which apparently tends in the opposite direction, viz. that a certain Lamprocles of Athens noticed that in the Mixo-lydian mode the Disjunctive Tone (**diazeuxis**) was at the upper end of the scale (**epi to oxy**), and reformed the scale accordingly. This must refer to an octave scale of the form *b c d e f g a b*, consisting of the two tetrachords *b-e* and *e-a*, and the tone *a-b*. Such an octave may or may not be in the Mixo-lydian key: it is certainly of the Mixo-lydian species (p. 57).

In estimating the value of this piece of evidence it is necessary to remark, in the first place, that the authority is no longer that of Aristoxenus, but of a certain Lysis, of whom nothing else seems to be known. That he was later than Aristoxenus is made probable by his way of describing the Mixo-lydian octave, viz. by reference to the notes in the Perfect System by which it is exemplified (Hypatê Hypatôn to Paramesê). In Aristoxenus, as we shall see (p. 31), the primitive octave (from Hypatê to Nêtê) is the only scale the notes of which are mentioned by name. But even if the notice is comparatively early, it is worth observing that the Mixo-lydian scale thus ascribed to Lamprocles consists of two tetrachords of the normal type, viz. with the semitone or **pyknon** at the lower end of the scale (Diatonic *e f g a*, Enharmonic *e e\* f a*). The difference is that they are conjunct, whereas in the primitive standard octave (*e—e*) the tetrachords are disjunct (*e-a b-e*). This, however, is a variety which is provided for by the tetrachord Synêmmenôn in the Perfect System, and which may have been allowed in the less complete scales of earlier times. In any case the existence of a scale of this particular form does not prove that the octaves of other species were recognised in the same way.

(2) In another passage (c. 6) Plutarch says of the ancient music of the cithara that it was characterised by perfect simplicity. It was not allowed, he tells us, to change the mode (**metapherein tas harmonias**) or the rhythm: for in the primitive lyrical compositions called 'Nomes' (**nomoi**) they preserved in each its proper pitch (**tên oikeian tasin**). Here the word **tasis** indicates that by **harmoniai** Plutarch (or the older author from whom he was quoting) meant particular *keys*. This is fully confirmed by the use of **tonos** in a passage a little further on (c. 8), where Plutarch gives an account of an innovation in this matter made by Sacadas of Argos (fl. 590 B.C.). 'There being three keys (**tonoi**) in the time of Polymnastus and Sacadas, viz. the Dorian, Phrygian and Lydian, it is said that Sacadas composed a strophe in each of these keys, and taught the chorus to sing them, the first in the Dorian, the second in the Phrygian, and the third in the Lydian key: and this composition was called the "three-part Nome" (**nomos trimerês**) on account of the change of key.' In Westphal's *Harmonik und Melopöie* (ed. 1863, p. 76, cp. p. 62) he explains this notice of the ancient modes (**harmoniai**, *Tonarten*), observing that the

word **tonos** is there used improperly for what the technical writers call **eidos tou dia pasôn**.

(3) In a somewhat similar passage of the same work (c. 19) Plutarch is contending that the fewness of the notes in the scales used by the early musicians did not arise from ignorance, but was characteristic of their art, and necessary to its peculiar ethos. Among other points he notices that the tetrachord Hypatôn was not used in Dorian music (**en tois Dôriois**), and this, he says, was not because they did not know of that tetrachord—for they used it in other keys (**tonoi**)—but they left it out in the Dorian key for the sake of preserving its ethos, the beauty of which they valued (**dia dê tên tou êthous phylakên aphêroun tou Dôriou tonou, timôntes to kalon autou**). Here again Westphal (*Aristoxenus*, p. 476) has to take **tonos** to mean **harmonia** or 'mode' (in his language *Tonart*, not *Transpositionsscala*). For in the view of those who distinguish **harmonia** from **tonos** it is the **harmonia** upon which the ethos of music depends. Plutarch himself had just been saying (in c. 17) that Plato preferred the Dorian **harmonia** on account of its grave and elevated character (**epei poly to semnon estin en tê Dôristi, tautên proutimêsen**). On the other hand the usual sense of **tonos** is supported by the consideration that the want of the tetrachord Hypatôn would affect the pitch of the scale rather than the succession of its intervals.

It seems to follow from a comparison of these three passages that Plutarch was not aware of any difference of meaning between the words **tonos** and **harmonia**, or any distinction in the scales of Greek music such as has been supposed to be conveyed by these words. Another synonym of **tonos** which becomes very common in the later writers on music is the word **tropos**. [6] In the course of the passage of Plutarch already referred to (*De Mus.* c. 17) it is applied to the Dorian mode, which Plutarch has just called **harmonia**. As **tropos** is always used in the later writers of the keys (**tonoi**) of Aristoxenus, this may be added to the places in which **harmonia** has the same meaning.

# § 13. Modes employed on different Instruments.

In the anonymous treatise on music published by Bellermann[7] (c. 28), we find the following statement regarding the use of the modes or keys in the scales of different instruments:

'The Phrygian mode (**harmonia**) has the first place on wind-instruments: witness the first discoverers—Marsyas, Hyagnis, Olympus—who were Phrygians. Players on the water-organ (**hydraulai**) use only six modes (**tropoi**), viz. Hyper-lydian, Hyper-ionian, Lydian, Phrygian, Hypo-lydian, Hypo-phrygian. Players on the cithara tune their instrument to these four, viz. Hyper-ionian, Lydian, Hypo-lydian, Ionian. Flute-players employ seven, viz. Hyper-aeolian, Hyper-ionian, Hypo-lydian, Lydian, Phrygian, Ionian, Hypo-phrygian. Musicians who concern themselves with orchestic (choral music) use seven, viz. Hyper-dorian, Lydian, Phrygian, Dorian, Hypo-lydian, Hypo-phrygian, Hypo-dorian.

In this passage it is evident that we have to do with keys of the scheme attributed to Aristoxenus, including the two (Hyper-aeolian and Hyper-lydian) which were said to have been added after his time. The number of scales mentioned is sufficient to prove that the reference is not to the seven species of the octave. Yet the word **harmonia** is used of these keys, and with it, seemingly as an equivalent, the word **tropos**.

Pollux (*Onom.* iv. 78) gives a somewhat different account of the modes used on the flute: **kai harmonia men aulêtikê Dôristi, Phrygisti, Lydios kai Iônikê, kai syntonos Lydisti hên Anthippos exeure**. But this statement, as has been already pointed out (p. 22), is a piece of antiquarian learning, and therefore takes no notice of the more recent keys, as Hyper-aeolian and Hyper-ionian, or even Hypo-phrygian (unless that is the Ionian of Pollux). The absence of Dorian from the list given by the *Anonymus* is curious: but it seems that at that time it was equally unknown to the cithara and the water-organ. There is therefore no reason to think that the two lists are framed with reference to different things. That is to say, **harmonia** in Pollux has the same meaning as **harmonia** in the *Anonymus*, and is equivalent to **tonos**.

# § 14. Recapitulation— harmonia and tonos.

The inquiry has now reached a stage at which we may stop to consider what result has been reached, especially in regard to the question whether the two words **harmonia** and **tonos** denote two sets of musical forms, or are merely two different names for the same thing. The latter alternative appears to be supported by several considerations.

1. From various passages, especially in Plato and Aristotle, it has been shown that the modes anciently called **harmoniai** differed in pitch, and that this difference in pitch was regarded as the chief source of the peculiar ethical character of the modes.

2. The list of **harmoniai** as gathered from the writers who treat of them, viz. Plato, Aristotle, and Heraclides Ponticus, is substantially the same as the list of **tonoi** described by Aristoxenus (p. 18): and moreover, there is an agreement in detail between the two lists which cannot be purely accidental. Thus Heraclides says that certain people had found out a new **harmonia**, the Hypo-phrygian; and Aristoxenus speaks of the Hypo-phrygian **tonos** as a comparatively new one. Again, the account which Aristoxenus gives of the Hypo-dorian **tonos** as a key immediately below the Dorian agrees with what Heraclides says of the Hypo-dorian **harmonia**, and also with the mention of Hypo-dorian and Hypo-phrygian (but not Hypo-lydian) in the Aristotelian *Problems*. Once more, the absence of Ionian from the list of **tonoi** in Aristoxenus is an exception which proves the rule: since the name of the Ionian **harmonia** is similarly absent from Aristotle.

3. The usage of the words **harmonia** and **tonos** is never such as to suggest that they refer to different things. In the earlier writers, down to and including Aristotle, **harmonia** is used, never **tonos**. In Aristoxenus and his school we find **tonos**, and in later writers **tropos**, but not **harmonia**. The few writers (such as Plutarch) who use both **tonos** and **harmonia** do not observe any consistent distinction between them. Those who (like Westphal) believe that there was a distinction, are obliged to admit that **harmonia** is occasionally used for **tonos** and conversely.

4. If a series of names such as Dorian, Phrygian, Lydian and the rest were applied to two sets of things so distinct from each other, and at the same time so important in the practice of music, as what we now call modes and keys, it is incredible that there should be no trace of the double usage. Yet our authors show no sense even of possible ambiguity. Indeed, they seem to prefer, in referring to modes or keys, to use the adverbial forms **dôristi**, **phrygisti**, &c., or the neuter **ta dôria**, **ta phrygia**, &c., where there is nothing to show whether 'mode' or 'key,' **harmonia** or **tonos**, is intended.

# § 15. The Systems of Greek Music.

The arguments in favour of identifying the primitive national Modes (**harmoniai**) with the **tonoi** or keys may be reinforced by some considerations drawn from the history and use of another ancient term, namely **systêma**.

A System (**systêma**) is defined by the Greek technical writers as a group or complex of intervals (**to ek pleionôn ê henos diastêmatôn synkeimenon** Ps. Eucl.). That is to say, any three or more notes whose *relative* pitch is fixed may be regarded as forming a particular System. If the notes are such as might be used in the same melody, they are said to form a *musical* System (**systêma emmeles**). As a matter of abstract theory it is evident that there are very many combinations of intervals which in this sense form a musical System. In fact, however, the variety of systems recognised in the theory of Greek music was strictly limited. The notion of a small number of scales, of a particular  compass, available for the use of the musician, was naturally suggested by the ancient lyre, with its fixed and conventional number of strings. The word for *string* (**chordê**) came to be used with the general sense of a *note* of music; and in this way the several strings of the lyre gave their names to the notes of the Greek gamut[8].

# § 16. The Standard Octachord System.

In the age of the great melic poets the lyre had no more than seven strings: but the octave was completed in the earliest times of which we have accurate information. The scale which is assumed as matter of common knowledge in the Aristotelian *Problems* and the *Harmonics* of Aristoxenus consists of eight notes, named as follows from their place on the lyre:

Nêtê    (**neatê** or **nêtê**, lit. 'lowest,' our 'highest').
Paranêtê    (**paranêtê**, 'next to Nêtê').
Tritê    (**tritê**, *i.e.* 'third' string).
Paramesê    (**paramesê** or **paramesos**, 'next to Mesê').
Mesê    (**mesê**, 'middle string').
Lichanos    (**lichanos**, *i.e.* 'forefinger' string).
Parhypatê    (**parypatê**).
Hypatê    (**hypatê**, lit. 'uppermost,' our 'lowest').

It will be seen that the conventional sense of high and low in the words **hypatê** and **neatê** was the reverse of the modern usage.

The musical scale formed by these eight notes consists of two *tetrachords* or scales of four notes, and a major tone. The lower of the tetrachords consists of the notes from Hypatê to Mesê, the higher of those from Paramesê to Nêtê: the interval between Mesê and Paramesê being the so-called *Disjunctive Tone* (**tonos diazeuktikos**). Within each tetrachord the intervals depend upon the *Genus* (**genos**). Thus the four notes just mentioned—Hypatê, Mesê, Paramesê, Nêtê—are the same for every genus, and accordingly are called the 'standing' or 'immoveable' notes (**phthongoi hestôtes, akinêtoi**), while the others vary with the genus, and are therefore 'moveable' (**pheromenoi**).

In the ordinary Diatonic genus the intervals of the tetrachords are, in the ascending order, semitone + tone + tone: *i.e.* Parhypatê is a semitone above Hypatê, and Lichanos a tone above Parhypatê. In the Enharmonic genus the intervals are two successive quarter-tones (**diesis**) followed by a ditone or major Third: consequently Parhypatê is only a quarter of a tone above Hypatê, and Lichanos again a quarter of a tone above Parhypatê. The group of three notes separated in this way by small intervals (viz. two successive quarter-tones) is called a **pyknon**. If we use an asterisk to denote that a note is raised a quarter of a tone, these two scales may be represented in modern notation as follows:

|  | *Diatonic.* |  |  | *Enharmonic.* |  |
|---|---|---|---|---|---|
| e | **Nêtê** | } | e | **Nêtê** | } |
| d | Paranêtê | } | c | Paranêtê | } |
| c | Tritê | } | b* | Tritê | } |
| b | **Paramesê** | } | b | **Paramesê** | } |
| a | **Mesê** |  | a | **Mesê** |  |
| g | Lichanos | } | f | Lichanos | } |
| f | Parhypatê | } | e* | Parhypatê | } |
| e | **Hypatê** | } | e | **Hypatê** | } |

(with πυκνόν marking the enharmonic groups)

πμχνον = pyknon

In the Chromatic genus and its varieties the division is of an intermediate kind. The interval between Lichanos and Mesê is more than one tone, but less than two: and the two other intervals, as in the enharmonic, are equal.

The most characteristic feature of this scale, in contrast to those of the modern Major and Minor, is the place of the small intervals (semitone or **pyknon**), which are always the lowest intervals of a tetrachord. It is hardly necessary to quote passages from Aristotle and Aristoxenus to show that this is the succession of intervals assumed by them. The question is asked in the Aristotelian *Problems* (xix. 4), why Parhypatê is difficult to sing, while Hypatê is easy, although there is only a diesis between them (**kaitoi diesis hekateras**). Again (*Probl.* xix. 47), speaking of the old heptachord scale, the writer says that the Paramesê was left out, and consequently the Mesê became the lowest note of the upper **pyknon**, *i.e.* the group of 'close' notes consisting of Mesê, Tritê, and Paranêtê. Similarly Aristoxenus (*Harm.* p. 23) observes that the 'space' of the Lichanos, *i.e.* the limit within which it varies in the different genera, is a tone while the space of the Parhypatê is only a diesis, for it is never nearer Hypatê than a diesis or further off than a semitone.

# § 17. Earlier Heptachord Scales.

Regarding the earlier seven-stringed scales which preceded this octave our information is scanty and somewhat obscure. The chief notice on the subject is the following passage of the Aristotelian *Problems*:

> *Probl.* xix. 47 **dia ti hoi archaioi heptachordous poiountes tas harmonias tên hypatên all' ou tên nêtên katelipon: hê ou tên hypatên** (leg. **nêtên**), **alla tên nyn paramesên kaloumenên aphêroun kai to toniaion diastêma; echrônto de tê eschatê mesê tou epi to oxy pyknou; did kai mesên autên prosêloreusan [hê] oti ên tou men anô tetrachordon teleutê, tou de katô archê, kai meson eiche logon tonô tôn akrôn?**

> 'Why did the ancient seven-stringed scales include Hypatê but not Nêtê? Or should we say that the note omitted was not Nêtê, but the present Paramesê and the interval of a tone (*i.e.* the disjunctive tone)? The Mesê, then, was the lowest note of the upper **pyknon**: whence the name **mesê**, because it was the end of the upper tetrachord and beginning of the lower one, and was in pitch the middle between the extremes.'

This clearly implies two conjunct tetrachords—

In another place (*Probl.* xix. 32) the question is asked, why the interval of the octave is called **dia pasôn**, not **di' oktô**,—as the Fourth is **dia tessarôn**, the Fifth **dia pente**. The answer suggested is that there were anciently seven strings, and that Terpander left out the Tritê and added the Nêtê. That is to say, Terpander increased the compass of the scale from the ancient two tetrachords to a full Octave; but he did not increase the number of strings to eight. Thus he produced a scale like the standard octave, but with one note wanting; so that the term **di oktô** was inappropriate.

Among later writers who confirm this account we may notice Nicomachus, p. 7 Meib. **mesê dia tessarôn pros amphotera en tê heptachordô kata to palaion diestôsa**: and p. 20 **tê toinyn archaiotropô lyra toutesti tê heptachordô, kata synaphên ek duo tetrachordôn synestôsê k.t.l.**

It appears then that two kinds of seven-stringed scales were known, at least by tradition: viz. (1) a scale composed of two conjunct tetrachords, and therefore of a compass less than an octave by one tone; and (2) a scale of the compass of an octave, but wanting a note, viz. the note above Mesê. The existence of this incomplete scale is interesting as a testimony to the force of the tradition which limited the number of strings to seven.

---

# § 18. The Perfect System.

The term 'Perfect System' (**systêma teleion**) is applied by the technical writers to a scale which is evidently formed by successive additions to the heptachord and octachord scales explained in the preceding chapter. It may be described as a combination of two scales, called the Greater and Lesser Perfect System.

The Greater Perfect System (**systêma teleion meizon**) consists of two octaves formed from the primitive octachord System by adding a tetrachord at each end of the scale. The new notes are named like those of the adjoining tetrachord of the original octave, but with the name of the tetrachord added by way of distinction. Thus below the original Hypatê we have a new tetrachord Hypatôn (**tetrachordon hypatôn**), the notes of which are accordingly called Hypatê Hypatôn, Parhypatê Hypatôn, and Lichanos Hypatôn: and similarly above Nêtê we have a tetrachord Hyperbolaiôn. Finally the octave downwards from Mesê is completed by the addition of a note appropriately called Proslambanomenos.

The Lesser Perfect System (**systêma teleion elasson**) is apparently based upon the ancient heptachord which consisted of two 'conjunct' tetrachords meeting in the Mesê. This scale was extended downwards in the  same way as the Greater System, and thus became a scale of three tetrachords and a tone.

These two Systems together constitute the Perfect and 'unmodulating' System (**systêma teleion ametabolon**), which may be represented in modern notation [9] as follows:

| | | | |
|---|---|---|---|
| a | Nêtê Hyperbolaiôn | } | Tetrachord |
| g | Paranêtê Hyperbolaiôn | } | Hyperbolaiôn |
| f | Tritê Hyperbolaiôn | } | |
| e | Nêtê Diezeugmenôn | | |
| d | Paranêtê Diezeugmenôn } | | |
| c | Tritê Diezeugmenôn | } | Tetrachord |
| b | Paramesê | } | Diezeugmenôn |
| d | Nêtê Synêmmenôn | } | |
| c | Paranêtê Synêmmenôn | } | Tetrachord |

| | | | |
|---|---|---|---|
| bb | Tritê Synêmmenôn | } | Synêmmenôn |
| a | Mesê | } | |
| g | Lichanos Mesôn | } | Tetrachord |
| f | Parhypatê Mesôn | } | Mesôn |
| e | Hypatê Mesôn | | |
| d | Lichanos Hypatôn | } | |
| c | Parhypatê Hypatôn | } | Tetrachord |
| b | Hypatê Hypatôn | } | Hypatôn |
| a | Proslambanomenos | | |

No account of the Perfect System is given by Aristoxenus, and there is no trace in his writings of an extension of the standard scale beyond the limits of the original octave. In one place indeed (*Harm.* p. 8, 12 Meib.) Aristoxenus promises to treat of Systems, 'and among them of the perfect System' (**peri te tôn allôn kai tou teleiou**). But we cannot assume that the phrase here had the technical sense which it bore in later writers. More probably it meant simply the octave scale, in contrast to the tetrachord and pentachord—a sense in which it is used by Aristides Quintilianus, p. 11 Meib. **synêmmenôn de eklêthê to holon systêma hoti tô prokeimenô teleiô tô mechri mesês synêptai**, 'the whole scale was called conjunct because it is conjoined to the complete scale that reaches up to Mesê' (*i.e.* the octave extending from Proslambanomenos to Mesê). So p. 16 **kai ha men autôn esti teleia, ha d' ou, atelê men tetrachordon, pentachordon, teleion de oktachordon.** This is a use of **teleios** which is likely enough to have come from Aristoxenus. The word was doubtless applied in each period to the most complete scale which musical theory had then recognised.

Little is known of the steps by which this enlargement of the Greek scale was brought about. We shall not be wrong in conjecturing that it was connected with the advance made from time to time in the form and compass of musical instruments [10]. Along with the lyre, which kept its primitive simplicity as the instrument of education and everyday use, the Greeks had the cithara (**kithara**), an enlarged and improved lyre, which, to judge from the representations on ancient monuments, was generally seen in the hands of professional players (**kitharôdoi**). The development of the cithara showed itself in the increase, of which we have good evidence even before the time of Plato, in the number of the strings. The poet Ion, the contemporary of Sophocles, was the author of an epigram on a certain ten-stringed lyre, which seems to have had a scale closely approaching that of the Lesser Perfect System [11]. A little later we hear of the comic poet Pherecrates attacking the musician Timotheus for various innovations tending to the loss of primitive simplicity, in particular the use of twelve strings [12]. According to a tradition mentioned by Pausanias, the Spartans condemned Timotheus because in his cithara he had added four strings to the ancient seven. The offending instrument was hung up in the Scias (the place of meeting of the Spartan assembly), and apparently was seen there by Pausanias himself (Paus. iii. 12, 8).

A similar or still more rapid development took place in the flute (**aulos**). The flute-player Pronomus of Thebes, who was said to have been one of the instructors of Alcibiades, invented a flute on which it was possible to play in all the modes. 'Up to his time,' says Pausanias (ix. 12, 5), 'flute-players had three forms of flute: with one they played Dorian music; a different set of flutes served for the Phrygian mode (**harmonia**); and the so-called Lydian was played on another kind again. Pronomus was the first who devised flutes fitted for every sort of mode, and played melodies different in mode on the same flute.' The use of the new invention soon became general, since in Plato's time the flute was the instrument most distinguished by the multiplicity of its notes: cp. Rep. p. 399 **ti de? aulopoious ê aulêtas paradexei eis tên polin? ê ou touto polychordotaton?** Plato may have had the invention of Pronomus in mind when he wrote these words.


With regard to the order in which the new notes obtained a place in the schemes of theoretical musicians we have no trustworthy information. The name **proslambanomenos**, applied to the lowest note of the Perfect System, points to a time when it was the last new addition to the scale. Plutarch in his work on the *Timaeus* of Plato (**peri tês en Timaiô psychogonias**) speaks of the Proslambanomenos as having been added in comparatively recent times (p. 1029 *c* **hoi de neôteroi ton proslambanomenon tonô diapheronta tês hypatês epi to bary taxantes to men holon diastêma dis dia pasôn epoiêsan**). The rest of the Perfect System he ascribes to 'the ancients' (**tous palaious ismen hypatas men dyo, treis de nêtas, mian de mesên kai mian paramesên tithemenous**). An earlier addition—perhaps the first made to the primitive octave—was a note called Hyperhypatê, which was a tone below the old Hypatê, in the place afterwards occupied on the Diatonic scale by Lichanos Hypatôn. It naturally disappeared when the tetrachord Hypatôn came into use. It is only mentioned by one author, Thrasyllus (quoted by Theon Smyrnaeus, cc. 35-36 [13]).

The notes of the Perfect System, with the intervals of the scale which they formed, are fully set out in the two treatises that pass under the name of the geometer Euclid, viz. the *Introductio Harmonica* and the *Sectio Canonis*. Unfortunately the authorship of both these works is doubtful [14]. All that we can say is that if the Perfect System was elaborated in the brief interval between the time of Aristotle and that of Euclid, the materials for it must have already existed in musical practice.

---

# § 19. Relation of System and Key.

Let us now consider the relation between this fixed or standard scale and the varieties denoted by the terms **harmonia** and **tonos**.

With regard to the **tonoi** or Keys of Aristoxenus we are not left in doubt. A system, as we have seen, is a series of notes whose *relative* pitch is fixed. The key in which the System is taken fixes the absolute pitch of the series. As Aristoxenus expresses it, the Systems are melodies set at the pitch of the different keys (**tous tonous, eph' hôn tithemena ta systêmata melôdeitai**). If then we speak of Hypatê or Mesê (just as when we speak of a moveable Do), we mean as many different notes as there are keys: but the Dorian Hypatê or the Lydian Mesê has an ascertained pitch. The Keys of Aristoxenus, in short, are so many transpositions of the scale called the Perfect System.

Such being the relation of the standard System to the key, can we suppose any different relation to have subsisted between the standard System and the ancient 'modes' known to Plato and Aristotle under the name of **harmoniai**?

It appears from the language used by Plato in the *Republic* that Greek musical instruments differed very much in the variety of modes or **harmoniai** of which they were susceptible. After Socrates has determined, in the passage quoted above (p. 7), that he will admit only two modes, the Dorian and Phrygian, he goes on to observe that the music of his state will not need a multitude of strings, or an instrument of all the modes (**panarmonion**) [15]. 'There will be no custom therefore for craftsmen who make triangles and harps and other instruments of many notes and many modes. How then about makers of the flute (**aulos**) and players on the flute? Has not the flute the greatest number of notes, and are not the scales which admit all the modes simply imitations of the flute? There remain then the lyre and the cithara for use in our city; and for shepherds in the country a syrinx (pan's pipes).' The lyre, it is plain, did not admit of changes of mode. The seven or eight strings were tuned to furnish the scale of one mode, not of more. What then is the relation between the mode or **harmonia** of a lyre and the standard scale or **systêma** which (as we have seen) was based upon the lyre and its primitive gamut?

If **harmonia** means 'key,' there is no difficulty. The scale of a lyre was usually the standard octave from Hypatê to Nêtê: and that octave might be in any one key. But if a mode is somehow characterised by a particular succession of intervals, what becomes of the standard octave? No one succession of intervals can then be singled out. It may be said that the standard octave is in fact the scale of a particular mode, which had come to be regarded as the type, viz. the Dorian. But there is no trace of any such prominence of the Dorian mode as this would necessitate. The philosophers who recognise its elevation and Hellenic purity are very far from implying that it had the chief place in popular regard. Indeed the contrary was evidently the case [16].

# § 20. Tonality of the Greek musical scale.

It may be said here that the value of a series of notes as the basis of a distinct mode—in the modern sense of the word—depends essentially upon the *tonality*. A single scale might yield music of different modes if the key-note were different. It is necessary therefore to collect the scanty notices which we possess bearing upon the tonality of Greek music. The chief evidence on the subject is a passage of the *Problems*, the importance of which was first pointed out by Helmholtz [17].

It is as follows:

> Arist. *Probl.* xix. 20: **Dia ti ean men tis tên mesên kinêsê hêmôn, harmosas tas allas chordas, kai chrêtai tô organô, ou monon hotan kata ton tês mesês genêtai phthongon lypei kai phainetai anarmoston, alla kai kata tên allên melôdian, ean de tên lichanon ê tina allon phthongon, tote phainetai diapherein monon hotan kakeinê tis chrêtai? ê eulogôs touto symbainei? panta gar ta chrêsta melê pollakis tê mesê chrêtai, kai pantes hoi agathoi poiêtai pykna pros tên mesên apantôsi, kan apelthôsi tachy epanerchontai, pros de allên houtôs oudemian. kathaper ek tôn logôn eniôn exairethentôn syndesmôn ouk estin ho logos Hellênikos, hoion to te kai to kai, enioi de outhen lypousi, dia to tois men anankaion einai chrêsthai pollakis, ei estai logos, tois de mê, houtô kai tôn phthongôn hê mesê hôsper syndesmos esti, kai malista tôn kalôn, dia to pleistakis enyparchein ton phthongon autês.**

'Why is it that if the Mesê is altered, after the other strings have been tuned, the instrument is felt to be out of tune, not only when the Mesê is sounded, but through the whole of the music,—whereas if the Lichanos or any other note is out of tune, it seems to be perceived only when that note is struck? Is it to be explained on the ground that all good melodies often use the Mesê, and all good composers resort to it frequently, and if they leave it soon return again, but do not make the same use of any other note? just as language cannot be Greek if certain conjunctions are omitted, such as **te** and **kai**, while others may be dispensed with, because the one class is necessary for language, but not the other: so with musical sounds the Mesê is a kind of 'conjunction,' especially of beautiful sounds, since it is most often heard among these.'

In another place (xix. 36) the question is answered by saying that the notes of a scale stand in a certain relation to the Mesê, which determines them with reference to it (**hê taxis hê hekastês êdê di' ekeinên**): so that the loss of the Mesê means the loss of the ground and unifying element of the scale (**arthentos tou aitiou tou hêrmosthai kai tou synechontos**) [18].

These passages imply that in the scale known to Aristotle, viz. the octave *e-e*, the Mesê *a* had the character of a Tonic or key-note. This must have been true *a fortiori* of the older seven-stringed scale, in which the Mesê united the two conjunct tetrachords. It was quite in accordance with this state of things that the later enlargement completed the octaves from Mesê downwards and upwards, so that the scale consisted of two octaves of the form *a-a*. As to the question how the Tonic character of the Mesê was shown, in what parts of the melody it was necessarily heard, and the like, we can but guess. The statement of the *Problems* is not repeated by any technical writer, and accordingly it does not appear that any rules on the subject had been arrived at. It is significant, perhaps, that the frequent use of the Mesê is spoken of as characteristic of *good* melody (**panta ta chrêsta melê pollakis tê mesê chrêtai**), as though tonality were a merit rather than a necessity.

Another passage of the *Problems* has been thought to show that in Greek music the melody ended on the Hypatê. The words are these (*Probl.* xix. 33):

> **Dia ti euarmostoteron apo tou oxeos epi to bary ê apo tou**

> **bareos epi to oxy; poteron hoti to apo tês archês ginetai archesthai? hê gar mesê kai hêgemôn oxytatê tou tetrachordou; to de ouk ap' archês all' apo teleutês.**

'Why is a descending scale more musical than an ascending one? Is it that in this order we begin with the beginning,—since the Mesê or leading note [19] is the highest of the tetrachord,—but with the reverse order we begin with the end?'

There is here no explicit statement that the melody ended on the Hypatê, or even that it began with the Mesê. In what sense, then, was the Mesê a 'beginning' (**archê**), and the Hypatê an 'end'? In Aristotelian language the word **archê** has various senses. It might be used to express the relation of the Mesê to the other notes as the basis or ground-work of the scale. Other passages, however, point to a simpler explanation, viz. that the order in question was merely conventional. In *Probl.* xix. 44 it is said that the Mesê is the beginning (**archê**) of one of the two tetrachords which form the ordinary octave scale (viz. the tetrachord Mesôn); and again in *Probl.* xix. 47 that in the old heptachord which consisted of two conjunct tetrachords (*e-a-d*) the Mesê (*a*) was the end of the upper tetrachord and the beginning of the lower one (**hoti ên tou men anô tetrachordou teleutê, tou de katô archê**). In this last passage it is evident that there is no reference to the beginning or end of the melody.

Another instance of the use of **archê** in connexion with the musical scale is to be found in the *Metaphysics* (iv. 11, p. 1018 *b* 26), where Aristotle is speaking of the different senses in which things may be prior and posterior:

> **Ta de kata taxin; tauta d' estin hosa pros ti hen hôrismenon diestêke kata ton logon, hoion parastatês tritostatou proteron, kai paranêtê nêtês; entha men gar ho koryphaios, entha de hê mesê archê.**

> 'Other things [are prior and posterior] in *order*: viz. those which are at a varying interval from some one definite thing; as the second man in the rank is prior to the third man, and the Paranêtê to the Nêtê: for in the one case the coryphaeus is the starting-point, in the other the Mesê.'

Here the Mesê is again the **archê** or beginning, but the order is the ascending one, and consequently the Nêtê is the end. The passage confirms what we have learned of the relative importance of the Mesê: but it certainly negatives any inference regarding the note on which the melody ended.

It appears, then, that the Mesê of the Greek standard System had the functions of a key-note in that System. In other words, the music was in the *mode* (using that term in the modern sense) represented by the octave *a-a* of the natural key—the Hypo-dorian or Common Species. We do not indeed know how the predominant character of the Mesê was shown—whether, for example, the melody ended on the Mesê. The supposed evidence for an ending on the Hypatê has been shown to be insufficient. But we may at least hold that as far as the Mesê was a key-note, so far the Greek scale was that of the modern Minor mode (descending). The only way of escape from this conclusion is to deny that the Mesê of *Probl.* xix. 20 was the note which we have understood by the term—the Mesê of the standard System. This, as we shall presently see, is the plea to which Westphal has recourse.

# § 21. The Species of a Scale.

The object of the preceding discussion has been to make it clear that the theory of a system of modes—in the modern sense of the word—finds no support from the earlier authorities on Greek music. There is, however, evidence to show that Aristoxenus, and perhaps other writers of the time, gave much thought to the varieties to be obtained by taking the intervals of a scale in different order. These varieties they spoke of as the *forms* or *species* (**schêmata, eidê**) of the interval which measured the compass of the scale in question. Thus, the interval of the Octave (**dia pasôn**) is divided into seven intervals, and these are, in the Diatonic genus, five tones and two semitones, in the Enharmonic two ditones, four quarter-tones, and a tone. As we shall presently see in detail, there are seven species of the Octave in each genus. That is to say, there are seven admissible octachord scales (**systêmata emmelê**), differing only in the succession of the intervals which compose them.

Further, there is evidence which goes to connect the seven species of the Octave with the Modes or **harmoniai**. In some writers these species are described under names which are familiar to us in their application to the modes. A certain succession of intervals is called the Dorian species of the Octave, another succession is called the Phrygian species, and so on for the Lydian, Mixo-lydian, Hypo-dorian, Hypo-phrygian, and Hypo-lydian. It seems natural to conclude that the species or successions of intervals so named were characteristic in some way of the modes which bore the same names, consequently that the modes were not keys, but modes in the modern sense of the term.

In order to estimate the value of this argument, it is necessary to ask, (1) how far back we can date the use of these names for the species of the Octave, and (2) in what degree the species of the Octave can be shown to have entered into the practice of music at any period. The answer to these questions must be gathered from a careful examination of all that Aristoxenus and other early writers say of the different musical scales in reference to the order of their intervals.

# § 22. The Scales as treated by Aristoxenus.

The subject of the musical scales (**systêmata**) is treated by Aristoxenus as a general problem, without reference to the scales in actual use. He complains that his predecessors dealt only with the octave scale, and only with the Enharmonic genus, and did not address themselves to the real question of the melodious sequence of intervals. Accordingly, instead of beginning with a particular scale, such as the octave, he supposes a scale of indefinite compass,—just as a mathematician postulates lines and surfaces of unlimited magnitude. His problem virtually is, given any interval known to the particular genus supposed, to determine what intervals can follow it on a musical scale, either ascending or descending. In the Diatonic genus, for example, a semitone must be followed by two tones, so as to make up the interval of a Fourth. In the Enharmonic genus the dieses or quarter-tones can only occur two together, and every such pair of dieses (**pyknon**) must be followed in the ascending order by a ditone, in the descending order by a ditone or a tone. By these and similar rules, which he deduces mathematically from one or two general principles of melody, Aristoxenus in effect determines all the possible scales of each genus, without restriction of compass or pitch [20]. But whenever he refers for the purpose of illustration to a scale in actual use, it is always the standard octave already described (from Hypatê to Nêtê), or a part of it. Thus nothing can be clearer than the distinction which he makes between the theoretically infinite scale, subject only to certain principles or laws determining the succession of intervals, and the eight notes, of fixed relative pitch, which constituted the gamut of practical music.

The passages in which Aristoxenus dwells upon the advance which he has made upon the methods of his predecessors are of considerable importance for the whole question of the species of the Octave. There are three or four places which it will be worth while to quote.

> 1. Aristoxenus, *Harm.* p. 2, 15 Meib.: **ta gar diagrammata autois tôn enarmoniôn** (harmoniôn MSS.) **ekkeitai monon systêmatôn, diatonôn d' ê chrômatikôn oudeis pôpoth' heôraken; kaitoi ta diagrammata g' autôn edêlou tên pasan tês melôdias taxin, en hois peri systêmatôn oktachordôn enarmoniôn** (harmoniôn MSS.) **monon elegon, peri de tôn allôn genôn te kai schêmatôn en autô te tô genei tontô kai tois loipois oud' epecheirei oudeis katamanthanein.**

'The diagrams of the earlier writers set forth Systems in the Enharmonic genus only, never in the Diatonic or Chromatic: and yet these diagrams professed to give the whole scheme of their music, and in them they treated of Enharmonic octave Systems only; of other genera and other forms of this or any genus no one attempted to discover anything.'

2. Ibid. p. 6, 20 Meib.: **tôn d' allôn katholou men kathaper emprosthen eipomen oudeis hêptai, henos de systêmatos Eratoklês epecheirêse kath' hen genos exarithmêsai ta schêmata tou dia pasôn apodeiktikôs tê periphora tôn diastêmatôn deiknys; ou katamathôn hoti, mê prosapodeichthentôn (qu. proapod.) tôn de tou dia pente schêmatôn kai tôn tou dia tessarôn pros de toutois kai tês syntheseôs autôn tis pot' esti kath' hên emmelôs syntithentai, pollaplasia tôn hepta symbainein gignesthai deiknytai.**

'The other Systems no one has dealt with by a general method: but Eratocles has attempted in the case of one System, in one genus, to enumerate the forms or *species* of the Octave, and to determine them mathematically by the periodic recurrence of the intervals: not perceiving that unless we have first demonstrated the forms of the Fifth and the Fourth, and the manner of their melodious combination, the forms of the Octave will come to be many more than seven.'

The 'periodic recurrence of intervals' here spoken of may be illustrated on the key-board of a piano. If we take successive octaves of white notes, *a-a*, *b-b*, and so on, we obtain each time a different order of intervals (*i.e.* the semitones occur in different places), until we reach *a-a* again, when the series begins afresh. In this way it is shown that only seven species of the Octave can be found on any particular scale. Aristoxenus shows how to prove this from first principles, viz. by analysing the Octave as the combination of a Fifth with a Fourth.

3. Ibid. p. 36, 29 Meib.: **tôn de systêmatôn tas diaphoras hoi men holôs ouk epecheiroun exarithmein, alla peri autôn monon tôn heptachordôn ha ekaloun harmonias tên episkepsin epoiounto, hoi de epicheirêsantes oudena tropon exêrithmounto.**

For **heptachordôn** Meibomius and other editors read **hepta oktachordôn**—a correction strongly suggested by the parallel words **systêmatôn oktachordôn** in the first passage quoted.

'Some did not attempt to enumerate the differences of the Systems, but confined their view to the seven octachord Systems which they called **harmoniai**; others who did make the attempt did not succeed.'

It appears from these passages that before the time of Aristoxenus musicians had framed diagrams or tables showing the division of the octave scale according to the Enharmonic genus: and that a certain Eratocles—of whom nothing else is known—had recognised seven forms or species of the octachord scale, and had shown how the order of the intervals in the several species passes through a sort of cycle. Finally, if the correction proposed in the third passage is right, the seven species of the Octave were somehow shown in the diagrams of which the first passage speaks. In what respect Eratocles failed in his treatment of the seven species can hardly be conjectured.

Elsewhere the diagrams are described by Aristoxenus somewhat differently, as though they exhibited a division into Enharmonic dieses or quarter-tones, without reference to the melodious character of the scale. Thus we find him saying—

4. *Harm.* p. 28 Meib.: **zêtêteon de to syneches ouch hôs hoi harmonikoi en tais tôn diagrammatôn katapyknôsesin apodidonai peirôntai, toutous apophainontes tôn phthongôn hexês allêlôn keisthai hois symbebêke to elachiston diastêma diechein aph' hautôn. ou gar to mê dynasthai dieseis oktô kai eikosin hexês melôdeisthai tês phônês estin, alla tên tritên diesin panta poiousa ouch hoia t' esti prostithenai.**

'We must seek continuity of succession, not as theoretical musicians do in filling up their diagrams with small intervals, making those notes successive which are separated from each other by the least interval. For it is not merely that the voice cannot sing twenty-eight successive dieses: with all its efforts it cannot sing a third diesis [21].'

This representation of the musical diagrams is borne out by the passage in the *Republic* in which Plato derides the experimental study of music:

*Rep.* p. 531 a **tas gar akouomenas au symphônias kai phthongous allêlois anametrountes anênyta, hôsper hoi astronomoi, ponousin. Nê tous theous, ephê, kai geloiôs ge, pyknômat' atta onomazontes kai paraballontes ta ôta, hoion ek geitonôn phônên thêreuomenoi, hoi men phasin eti katakouein en mesô tina êchên kai smikrotaton einai touto diastêma, hô metrêteon, hoi de k.t.l.**

Here Socrates is insisting that the theory of music should be studied as a branch of mathematics, not by observation of the sounds and concords actually heard, about which musicians spend toil in vain. 'Yes,' says Glaucon, 'they talk of the close-fitting of intervals, and put their ears down to listen for the smallest possible interval, which is then to be the measure.' The smallest interval was of course the Enharmonic diesis or quarter of a tone, and this accordingly was the measure or unit into which the scale was divided. A group of notes separated by a diesis was called 'close' (**pyknon**, or a **pyknôma**), and the filling up of the scale in that way was therefore a **katapyknôsis tou diagrammatos**—a filling up with 'close-set' notes, by the division of every tone into four equal parts.

An example of a diagram of this kind has perhaps survived in a comparatively late writer, viz. Aristides Quintilianus, who gives a scale of two octaves, one divided into twenty-four dieses, the next into twelve semitones (*De Mus.* p. 15 Meib.). The characters used are not otherwise known, being quite different from the ordinary notation: but the nature of the diagram is plain from the accompanying words: **hautê estin hê para tois archaiois kata dieseis harmonia, heôs κδ dieseôn to proteron diagousa dia pasôn, to deuteron dia tôn hêmitoniôn auxêsasa**: 'this is the **harmonia** (division of the scale) according to dieses in use among the ancients, carried in the case of the first octave as far as twenty-four dieses, and dividing the second into semitones [22].'

The phrase **hê kata dieseis harmonia**, used for the division of an octave scale into quarter-tones, serves to explain the statement of Aristoxenus (in the third of the passages above quoted) that the writers who treated of octave Systems called them 'harmonies' (**ha ekaloun harmonias**). That statement has usually been taken to refer to the ancient Modes called **harmoniai** by Plato and Aristotle, and has been used accordingly as proof that the scales of these Modes were based upon the different species (**eidê**) of the Octave. But the form of the reference—'which *they called* **harmoniai**'—implies some forgotten or at least unfamiliar use of the word by the older technical writers. It is very much more probable that the **harmoniai** in question are divisions of the octave scale, as shown in theoretical diagrams, and had no necessary connexion with the Modes. Apparently some at least of these diagrams were not musical scales, but tables of all the notes in the compass of an octave; and the Enharmonic diesis was used, not merely on account of the importance of that genus, but because it was the smallest interval, and therefore the natural unit of measurement [23].

The use of **harmonia** as an equivalent for 'System' or 'division of the scale' appears in an important passage in Plato's *Philebus* (p. 17): **all', ô phile,**

- 43 -

epeidan labês ta diastêmata hoposa esti ton arithmon tês phônês oxytêtos te peri kai barytêtos, kai hopoia, kai tous horous tôn diastêmatôn, kai ta ek toutôn hosa systêmata gegonen, ha katidontes hoi prosthen paredosan hêmin tois hepomenois ekeinois kalein auta harmonias, k.t.l. In this passage,—which has an air of technical accuracy not usual in Plato's references to music (though perhaps characteristic of the *Philebus*),—there is a close agreement with the technical writers, especially Aristoxenus. The main thought is the application of limit or measure to matter which is given as unlimited or indefinite—the distinction drawn out by Aristoxenus in a passage quoted below (p. 81). The treatment of the term 'System' is notably Aristoxenean (cp. *Harm.* p. 36 **ta systêmata theôrêsai posa te esti kai poia atta, kai pôs ek te tôn diastêmatôn kai phthongôn synestêkota**). Further, the use of **harmonia** for **systêma**, or rather of the plural **harmoniai** for the **systêmata** observed by the older musical theorists, is exactly what is noticed by Aristoxenus as if it were more or less antiquated. Even in the time of Plato it appears as a word of traditional character (**hoi prosthen paredosan**), his own word being **systêma**. It need not be said that there is no such hesitation, either in Plato or in Aristotle, about the use of **harmoniai** for the modes.

The same use of **harmonia** is found in the Aristotelian *Problems* (xix. 26), where the question is asked, **dia ti mesê kaleitai en tais harmoniais, tôn de oktô ouk esti meson**, *i.e.* how can we speak of the Mesê or 'middle note' of a scale of eight notes?

We have now reviewed all the passages in Aristoxenus which can be thought to bear upon the question whether the **harmoniai** or Modes of early Greek music are the same as the **tonoi** or Keys discussed by Aristoxenus himself. The result seems to be that we have found nothing to set against the positive arguments for the identification already urged. It may be thought, perhaps, that the variety of senses ascribed to the word **harmonia** goes beyond what is probable. In itself however the word meant simply 'musical scale [24].' The Pythagorean use of it in the sense of 'octave scale,' and the very similar use in reference to diagrams which represented the division of that scale, were antiquated in the time of Aristoxenus. The sense of 'key' was doubtless limited in the first instance to the use in conjunction with the names Dorian, &c., which suggested a distinction of pitch. From the meaning 'Dorian scale' to 'Dorian key' is an easy step. Finally, in reference to genus **harmonia** meant the Enharmonic scale. It is not surprising that a word with so many meanings did not keep its place in technical language, but was replaced by unambiguous words, viz. **tonos** in one sense, **systêma** in another, **genos enarmonion** in a third. Naturally, too, the more precise terms would be first employed by technical writers.

# § 23. The Seven Species.

(See the Appendix, Table I.)

In the *Harmonics* of Aristoxenus an account of the seven species of the Octave followed the elaborate theory of Systems already referred to (p. 48), and doubtless exhibited the application of that general theory to the particular cases of the Fourth, Fifth, and Octave. Unfortunately the existing manuscripts have only preserved the first few lines of this chapter of the Aristoxenean work (p. 74, ll. 10-24 Meib.).


The next source from which we learn anything of this part of the subject is the pseudo-Euclidean *Introductio Harmonica*. The writer enumerates the species of the Fourth, the Fifth, and the Octave, first in the Enharmonic and then in the Diatonic genus. He shows that if we take Fourths on a Diatonic scale, beginning with Hypatê Hypatôn (our *b*), we get successively *b c d e* (a scale with the intervals ½ 1 1), *c d e f* (1 1 ½) and *d e f g* (1 ½ 1). Similarly on the Enharmonic scale we get—

Hypatê Hypatôn to **Hypatê Mesôn**   *b*   *b\**   *c*   *e*   (¼   ¼   2 )

Parhypatê   "   "   Parhypatê   "   *b\**   *c*   *e*   *e\**   (¼   2   ¼)

Lichanos   "   "   Lichanos   "   *c*   *e*   *e\**   *f*   (2   ¼   ¼)

In the case of the Octave the species is distinguished on the Enharmonic scale by the place of the tone which separates the tetrachords, the so-called Disjunctive Tone (**tonos diazeuktikos**). Thus in the octave from Hypatê Hypatôn to Paramesê (*b-b*) this tone (*a-b*) is the highest interval; in the next octave, from Parhypatê Hypatôn to Tritê Diezeugmenôn (*c-c*), it is the second highest; and so on. These octaves, or species of the Octave, the writer goes on to tell us, were anciently called by the same names as the seven oldest Keys, as follows:

| | | | | | | | | |
|---|---|---|---|---|---|---|---|---|
| Mixo-lydian | *b - b* | ¼ | ¼ | 2 | ¼ | ¼ | 2 | 1 |
| Lydian | *b\*- b\** | ¼ | 2 | ¼ | ¼ | 2 | 1 | ¼ |
| Phrygian | *c - c* | 2 | ¼ | ¼ | 2 | 1 | ¼ | ¼ |
| Dorian | *e - e* | ¼ | ¼ | 2 | 1 | ¼ | ¼ | 2 |
| Hypo-lydian | *e\*- e\** | ¼ | 2 | 1 | ¼ | ¼ | 2 | ¼ |
| Hypo-phrygian | *f - f* | 2 | 1 | ¼ | ¼ | 2 | ¼ | ¼ |

| Hypo-dorian | $a - a$ | 1 | ¼ | ¼ | 2 | ¼ | ¼ | 2 |

On the Diatonic scale, according to the same writer, the species of an Octave is distinguished by the places of the two semitones. Thus in the first species, *b-b*, the semitones are the first and fourth intervals (*b-c* and *e-f*): in the second, *c-c*, they are the third and the seventh, and so on. He does not however say, as he does in the case of the Enharmonic scale, that these species were known by the names of the Keys. This statement is first made by Gaudentius (p. 20 Meib.), a writer of unknown date. If we adopt it provisionally, the species of the Diatonic octave will be as follows:

| [Mixo-lydian] | $b - b$ | ½ | 1 | 1 | ½ | 1 | 1 | 1 |
| [Lydian] | $c - c$ | 1 | 1 | ½ | 1 | 1 | 1 | ½ |
| [Phrygian] | $d - d$ | 1 | ½ | 1 | 1 | 1 | ½ | 1 |
| [Dorian] | $e - e$ | ½ | 1 | 1 | 1 | ½ | 1 | 1 |
| [Hypo-lydian] | $f - f$ | 1 | 1 | 1 | ½ | 1 | 1 | ½ |
| [Hypo-phrygian] | $g - g$ | 1 | 1 | ½ | 1 | 1 | ½ | 1 |
| [Hypo-dorian] | $a - a$ | 1 | ½ | 1 | 1 | ½ | 1 | 1 |

# § 24. Relation of the Species to the Keys.

Looking at the octaves which on our key-board, as on the Greek scale, exhibit the several species, we cannot but be struck with the peculiar relation in which they stand to the Keys. In the tables given above the keys stand in the order of their pitch, from the Mixo-lydian down to the Hypo-dorian: the species of the same names follow the reverse order, from *b-b* upwards to *a-a*. This, it is obvious, cannot be an accidental coincidence. The two uses of this famous series of names cannot have originated independently. Either the naming of the species was founded on that of the keys, or the converse relation obtained between them. Which of these two uses, then, was the original and which the derived one? Those who hold that the species were the basis of the ancient Modes or **harmoniai** must regard the keys as derivative. Now Aristoxenus tells us, in one of the passages just quoted, that the seven species had long been recognised by theorists. If the scheme of keys was founded upon the seven species, it would at once have been complete, both in the number of the keys and in the determination of the intervals between them. But Aristoxenus also tells us that down to his time there were only six keys,—one of them not yet generally recognised,—and that their relative pitch was not settled. Evidently then the keys, which were scales in practical use, were still incomplete when the species of the Octave had been worked out in the theory of music.

If on the other hand we regard the names Dorian, &c. as originally applied to keys, we have only to suppose that these names were extended to the species after the number of seven keys had been completed. This supposition is borne out by the fact that Aristoxenus, who mentions the seven species as well known, does not give them names, or connect them with the keys. This step was apparently taken by some follower of Aristoxenus, who wished to connect the species of the older theorists with the system of keys which Aristoxenus had perfected.

The view now taken of the seven species is supported by the whole treatment of musical scales (**systêmata**) as we find it in Aristoxenus. That treatment from first to last is purely abstract and theoretical. The rules which Aristoxenus lays down serve to determine the sequence of intervals, but are not confined to scales of any particular compass. His Systems, accordingly, are not scales in practical use: they are parts taken anywhere on an ideal unlimited scale. And the seven species of the Octave are regarded by Aristoxenus as a scheme of the same abstract order. They represent the earlier teaching on which he had improved. He condemned that teaching for its want of generality, because it was confined to the compass of the Octave and to the Enharmonic genus, and also because it rested on no principles that would necessarily limit the species of the Octave to seven. On the other hand the diagrams of the earlier musicians were unscientific, in the opinion of Aristoxenus, on the ground that they divided the scale into a succession of quarter-tones. Such a division, he urged, is impossible in practice and musically wrong (**ekmeles**). All this goes to show that the earlier treatment of Systems, including the seven Species, had the same theoretical character as his own exposition. The only System which he recognises for practical purposes is the old standard octave, from Hypatê to Nêtê: and that System, with the enlargements which turned it into the Perfect System, kept its ground with all writers of the Aristoxenean school.

Even in the accounts of the pseudo-Euclid and the later writers, who treat of the Species of the Octave under the names of the Keys, there is much to show that the species existed chiefly or wholly in musical theory. The seven species of the Octave are given along with the three species of the Fourth and the four species of the Fifth, neither of which appear to have had any practical application. Another indication of this may be seen in the seventh or Hypo-dorian species, which was also called Locrian and Common (ps. Eucl. p. 16 Meib.). Why should this species have more than one name? In the Perfect System it is  singular in being exemplified by two different octaves, viz. that from Proslambanomenos to Mesê, and that from Mesê to Nêtê Hyperbolaiôn. Now we have seen that the higher the octave which represents a species, the lower the key of the same name. In this case, then, the upper of the two octaves answers to the Hypo-dorian key, and the lower to the Locrian. But if the species has its two names from these two keys, it follows that the names of the species are derived from the keys. The fact that the Hypo-dorian or Locrian species was also called Common is a further argument to the same purpose. It was doubtless 'common' in the sense that it characterised the two octaves which made up the Perfect System. Thus the Perfect System was recognised as the really important scale.

Another consideration, which has been overlooked by Westphal and those who follow him, is the difference between the species of the Octave in the several genera, especially the difference between the Diatonic and the Enharmonic. This is not felt as a difficulty with all the species. Thus the so-called Dorian octave *e-e* is in the Enharmonic genus *e e\* f a b b\* c e*, a scale which may be regarded as the Diatonic with *g* and *d* omitted, and the semitones divided. But the Phrygian *d-d* cannot pass in any such way into the Enharmonic Phrygian *c e e\* f a b b\* c*, which answers rather to the Diatonic scale of the species *c-c* (the Lydian). The scholars who connect the ancient Modes with the species generally confine themselves to octaves of the Diatonic genus. In this they are supported by later Greek writers—notably, as we shall see, by Ptolemy—and by the analogy of the mediaeval Modes or Tones. But on the other side we have the repeated complaints  of Aristoxenus that the earlier theorists confined themselves to Enharmonic octave scales. We have also the circumstance that the writer or compiler of the pseudo-Euclidean treatise, who is our earliest authority for the names of the species, gives these names for the Enharmonic genus only. Here, once more, we feel the difference between theory and practice. To a theorist there is no great difficulty in the terms Diatonic Phrygian and Enharmonic Phrygian meaning essentially different things. But the 'Phrygian Mode' in practical music must have been a tolerably definite musical form.

# § 25. The Ethos of Music.

From Plato and Aristotle we have learned some elements of what may be called the gamut of sensibility. Between the higher keys which in Greece, as in Oriental countries generally, were the familiar vehicle of passion, especially of the passion of grief, and the lower keys which were regarded, by Plato at least, as the natural language of ease and license, there were keys expressive of calm and balanced states of mind, free from the violent extremes of pain and pleasure. In some later writers on music we find this classification reduced to a more regular form, and clothed in technical language. We find also, what is still more to our purpose, an attempt to define more precisely the musical forms which answered to the several states of temper or emotion.

Among the writers in question the most instructive is Aristides Quintilianus. He discusses the subject of musical ethos under the first of the usual seven heads, that which deals with sounds or notes (**peri phthongôn**). Among the distinctions to be drawn in regard to notes he reckons that of ethos: the ethos of notes, he says, is different as they are higher or lower, and also as they are in the place of a Parhypatê or in the place of a Lichanos (p. 13 Meib. **hetera gar êthê tois oxyterois, hetera tois baryterois epitrechei, kai hetera men parypatoeidesin, hetera de lichanoeidesin**). Again, under the seventh head, that of **melopoiia** or composition, he treats of the 'regions of the voice' (**topoi tês phônês**). There are three kinds of composition, he tells us (p. 28), viz. that which is akin to Hypatê (**hypatoeidês**), that which is akin to Mesê (**mesoeidês**), and that which is akin to Nêtê (**nêtoeidês**). The first part of the art of composition is the choice (**lêpsis**) which the musician is able to make of the region of the voice to be employed (**lêpsis men di' hês heuriskein tô mousikô perigignetai apo poiou tês phônês to systêma topou poiêteon, poteron hypatoeidous ê tôn loipôn tinos**). He then proceeds to connect these regions, or different parts of the musical scale, with different branches of lyrical poetry. 'There are three styles of musical composition (**tropoi tês melopoiias**), viz. the Nomic, the Dithyrambic, and the Tragic; and of these the Nomic is netoid, the Dithyrambic is mesoid, and the Tragic is hypatoid.... They are called styles (**tropoi**) because according to the melody adopted they express the ethos of the mind. Thus it happens that composition (**melopoiia**) may differ in *genus*, as Enharmonic, Chromatic: in *System*, as Hypatoid, Mesoid, Netoid: in *key*, as Dorian, Phrygian: in *style*, as Nomic, Dithyrambic: in *ethos*, as we call one kind of composition "contracting" (**systaltikê**), viz. that by which we move painful feelings; another "expanding" (**diastaltikê**), that by which we arouse the spirit (**thymos**); and another "middle" (**mesê**), that by which we bring round the soul to calmness.'

This passage does not quite explicitly connect the three kinds of ethos—the diastaltic, the systaltic, the intermediate—with the three regions of the voice; but the connexion was evidently implied, and is laid down in express terms in the pseudo-Euclidean *Introductio* (p. 21 Meib.). According to this Aristoxenean writer, 'the diastaltic ethos of musical composition is that which expresses grandeur and manly elevation of soul (**megaloprepeia kai diarma psychês andrôdes**), and heroic actions; and these are employed by tragedy and all poetry that approaches the tragic type. The systaltic ethos is that by which the soul is brought down into a humble and unmanly frame; and such a disposition will be fitting for amatory effusions and dirges and lamentations and the like. And the hesychastic or tranquilly disposed ethos (**hêsychastikon êthos**) of musical composition is that which is followed by calmness of soul and a liberal and peaceful disposition: and this temper will fit hymns, paeans, laudations, didactic poetry and the like.' It appears then that difference in the 'place' (**topos**) of the notes employed in a composition—difference, that is to say, of pitch—was the element which chiefly determined its ethos, and (by consequence) which distinguished the music appropriate to the several kinds of lyrical poetry.

A slightly different version of this piece of theory is preserved in the anonymous treatise edited by Bellermann (§§ 63, 64), where the 'regions of the voice' are said to be four in number, viz. the three already mentioned, and a fourth which takes its name from the tetrachord Hyperbolaiôn (**topos hyperboloeidês**). In the same passage the boundaries of the several regions are laid down by reference to the keys. 'The lowest or hypatoid region reaches from the Hypo-dorian Hypatê Mesôn to the Dorian Mesê; the intermediate or mesoid region from the Phrygian Hypatê Mesôn to the Lydian Mesê; the netoid region from the Lydian Mesê to the Nêtê Synemmenôn; the hyperboloid region embracing all above the last point.' The text of this passage is uncertain; but the general character of the **topoi** or regions of the voice is clearly enough indicated.

The three regions are mentioned in the catechism of Bacchius (p. 11 Meib.): **topous** (MSS. **tropous**) **de tês phônês posous legomen einai? treis. tinas? toutous; oxyn, meson, baryn.** The varieties of ethos also appear (p. 14 Meib.): **hê de metabolê kata êthos? hotan ek tapeinou eis megaloprepes; ê ex hêsychou kai synnou eis parakekinêkos.** 'What is change of ethos? when a change is made from the humble to the magnificent; or from the tranquil and sober to violent emotion.'

When we compare the doctrine of musical ethos as we find it in these later writers with the indications to be gathered from Plato and Aristotle, the chief difference appears to be that we no longer hear of the ethos of particular modes, but only of that of three or (at the most) four portions of the scale. The principle of the division, it is evident, is simply difference of pitch. But if that was the basis of the ethical effect of music in later times, the circumstance goes far to confirm us in the conclusion that it was the pitch of the music, rather than any difference in the succession of the intervals, that principally determined the ethical character of the older modes.

---

# § 26. The Ethos of the Genera and Species.

Although the pitch of a musical composition—as these passages confirm us in believing—was the chief ground of its ethical character, it cannot be said that no other element entered into the case.

In the passage quoted above from Aristides Quintilianus (p. 13 Meib.) it is said that ethos depends first on pitch (**hetera êthê tois oxyterois, hetera tois baryterois**), and secondly on the moveable notes, that is to say, on the *genus*. For that is evidently involved in the words that follow: **kai hetera men parypatoeidesin, hetera de lichanoeidesin.** By **parypatoeideis** and **lichanoeideis** he means all the moveable notes (**phthongoi pheromenoi**): the first are those which hold the place of Parhypatê in their tetrachord, viz. the notes called Parhypatê or Tritê: the second are similarly the notes called Lichanos or Paranêtê. These moveable notes, then, give an ethos to the music because they determine the genus of the scale. Regarding the particular ethos belonging to the different genera, there is a statement of the same author (p. 111) to the effect that the Diatonic is masculine and austere (**arrhenôpon d' esti kai austêroteron**), the Chromatic sweet and plaintive (**hêdiston te kai goeron**), the Enharmonic stirring and pleasing (**diegertikon d' esti touto kai êpion**). The criticism doubtless came from some earlier source.

Do we ever find ethos attributed to this or that *species* of the Octave? I can find no passage in which this source of ethos is indicated. Even Ptolemy, who is the chief authority (as we shall see) for the value of the species, and who makes least of mere difference of pitch, recognises only two forms of modulation in the course of a melody, viz. change of genus and change of pitch [25].

# § 27. The Musical Notation.

As the preceding argument turns very much upon the practical importance of the scale which we have been discussing, first as the single octave from the original Hypatê to Nêtê, then in its enlarged form as the Perfect System, it may be worth while to show that some such scale is implied in the history of the Greek musical notation.

The use of written characters (**sêmeia**) to represent the sounds of music appears to date from a comparatively early period in Greece. In the time of Aristoxenus the art of writing down a melody (**parasêmantikê**) had come to be considered by some persons identical with the science of music (**harmonikê**),—an error which Aristoxenus is at some pains to refute. It is true that the authorities from whom we derive our knowledge of the Greek notation are post-classical. But the characters themselves, as we shall presently see, furnish sufficient evidence of their antiquity.

The Greek musical notation is curiously complicated. There is a double set of characters, one for the note assigned to the singer, the other for those of the lyre or other instrument. The notes for the voice are obviously derived from the letters of the ordinary Ionic alphabet, multiplied by the use of accents and other diacritical marks. The instrumental notes were first explained less than thirty years ago by Westphal. In his work *Harmonik und Melopöie der Griechen* (c. viii *Die Semantik*) he showed, in a manner as conclusive as it is ingenious, that they were originally taken from the first fourteen letters of an alphabet of archaic type, akin to the alphabets found in certain parts of Peloponnesus. Among the letters which he traces, and which point to this conclusion, the most-significant are the digamma, the primitive crooked iota ⌐, and two forms of lambda, ≺ and ⊦, the latter of which is peculiar to the alphabet of Argos. Of the other characters ⅄, which stands for alpha, is best derived from the archaic form ⋈. For beta we find ⊏, which may come from an archaic form of the letter[26]. The character ⊓, as Westphal shows, is for ⅂, or delta with part of one side left out. Similarly the ancient ⊙, when the circle was incomplete, yielded the character C. The crooked iota (⌐) appears as ⊓. The two forms of lambda serve for different notes, thus bringing the number of symbols up to fifteen. Besides these there are two characters, ⊐ and Ɛ, which cannot be derived in the same way from any alphabet. As they stand for the lowest notes of the scale, they are probably an addition, later than the rest of the system. At the upper end,

- 54 -

again, the scale is extended by the simple device of using the same characters for notes an octave higher, distinguishing them in this use by an accent. The original fifteen characters, with the letters from which they are derived, and the corresponding notes in the modern musical scale, are as follows:

| H | ʰ | E | ⊢ | Γ | ⋏ | F | C | K | ⊓ | < | ⊏ | N | Z | ⋎ |
|---|---|---|---|---|---|---|---|---|---|---|---|---|---|---|
| $\eta$ | $\iota$ | $\epsilon$ | $\lambda^1$ | $\gamma$ | $\mu$ | $F$ | $\theta$ | $\kappa$ | $\delta$ | $\lambda^2$ | $\beta$ | $\nu$ | $\zeta$ | $\alpha$ |
| *a* | *b* | *c* | *d* | *e* | *f* | *g* | *a* | *b* | *c* | *d* | *e* | *f* | *g* | *a* |

These notes, it will be seen, compose two octaves of the Diatonic scale, identical with the two octaves of the Greater Perfect System. They may be regarded as answering to the white notes of the modern keyboard,—those which form the complete scale in the so-called 'natural' key.

The other notes, viz. those which are required not only in different keys of the Diatonic scale, but also in all Enharmonic and Chromatic scales, are represented by the same characters modified in some simple way. Usually a character is turned half round backwards to raise it by one small interval (as from Hypatê to Parhypatê), and reversed to raise it by both (Hypatê to Lichanos). Thus the letter epsilon, **E**, stands for our *c*: and accordingly **Ш** (**E** anestrammenon or hyption) stands for *c\**, and **Ǝ** (**E** apestrammenon) for *c♯*. The Enharmonic scale *c-c\*-c♯-f* is therefore written

**E Ш Ǝ ⋏**, the two modifications of the letter **E** representing the two 'moveable' notes of the tetrachord. Similarly we have the triads

**ʰ ⊥ �ʜ**, **⊢ ⊥ ⊣**, **F L ⅂**, **⋏ ⤙ ⋎ C ∪ ⊃**, **K ⅄ ⋊** , **< v >** , **⊏ ⊔ ⊐** . As some letters do not admit of this kind of differentiation, other methods are employed. Thus Δ is made to yield the forms **⊓** (for **7**) **∠**Δ: from H (or B) are obtained the forms **ⴑ** and **ꓤ** : and from Z (or I]) the forms **ⴠ** and **ⴞ** . The modifications of **N** are / and \: those of **⋎** are **ⴠ** and **ⴞ** .

The method of writing a Chromatic tetrachord is the same, except that the higher of the two moveable notes is marked by a bar or accent. Thus the tetrachord *c c♯ d f* is written **E Ш Ǝ ⋏** .

In the Diatonic genus we should have expected that the original characters would have been used for the tetrachords *b c d e* and *e f g a*; and that in other tetrachords the second note, being a semitone above the first, would have been represented by a reversed letter (**gramma apestrammenon**). In fact, however, the Diatonic Parhypatê and Tritê are written with the same character as the Enharmonic. That is to say, the tetrachord *b c d e* is not

written **ㅏ ㅌ ㅏ Ⲅ** , but **ㅏ ㅗ ㅏ Ⲅ** : and *d eb f g* is not

**ㅏ ㅓ ⋏ ꟻ** , but **ㅏ ㅓ ⋏ ꟻ**
              u ‡          .

Let us now consider how this scheme of symbols is related to the Systems already described and the Keys in which those Systems may be set (**tonoi eph' hôn tithemena ta systêmata melôdeitai**).

The fifteen characters, it has been noticed, form two diatonic octaves. It will appear on a little further examination that the scheme must have been constructed with a view to these two octaves. The successive notes are not expressed by the letters of the alphabet in their usual order (as is done in the case of the vocal notes). The highest note is represented by the first letter, **A**: and then the remaining fourteen notes are taken in pairs, each with its octave: and each of the pairs of notes is represented by two successive letters—the two forms of lambda counting as one such pair of letters. Thus:

## The higher and lower *e* are denoted by $\beta$ and $\gamma$

| | | | | | | | | |
|---|---|---|---|---|---|---|---|---|
| ,, | ,, | ,, | *c* | ,, | ,, | $\delta$ | ,, | $\epsilon$ |
| ,, | ,, | ,, | *g* | ,, | ,, | $F$ | ,, | $\zeta$ |
| ,, | ,, | ,, | *a* | ,, | ,, | $\eta$ | ,, | $\theta$ |
| ,, | ,, | ,, | *b* | ,, | ,, | $\iota$ | ,, | $\kappa$ |
| ,, | ,, | ,, | *d* | ,, | ,, | $\lambda^1$ | ,, | $\lambda^2$ |
| ,, | ,, | ,, | *f* | ,, | ,, | $\mu$ | ,, | $\nu$ |

On this plan the alphabetical order of the letters serves as a series of links connecting the highest and lowest notes of every one of the seven octaves that can be taken on the scale. It is evident that the scheme cannot have grown up by degrees, but is the work of an inventor who contrived it for the practical requirements of the music of his time.

Two questions now arise, which it is impossible to separate. What is the scale or System for which the notation was originally devised? And how and when was the notation adapted to exhibit the several keys in which any such System might be set?

The enquiry must start from the remarkable fact that the two octaves represented by the fifteen original letters are in the *Hypo-lydian* key—the key which down to the time of Aristoxenus was called the Hypo-dorian. Are we to suppose that the scheme was devised in the first instance for that key only? This assumption forms the basis of the ingenious and elaborate theory by which M. Gevaert explains the development of the notation (*Musique de l'Antiquité*, t. I. pp. 244 ff.). It is open to the obvious objection that the Hypo-lydian (or Hypo-dorian) cannot have been the oldest key. M. Gevaert meets this difficulty by supposing that the original scale was in the Dorian key, and that subsequently, from some cause the nature of which we cannot guess, a change of pitch took place by which the Dorian scale became a semitone higher. It is perhaps simpler to conjecture that the original Dorian became split up, so to speak, into two keys by difference of local usage, and that the lower of the two came to be called Hypo-dorian, but kept the original notation. A more serious difficulty is raised by the high antiquity which M. Gevaert assigns to the Perfect System. He supposes that the inventor of the notation made use of an instrument (the *magadis*) which 'magadised' or repeated the notes an octave higher. But this would give us a repetition of the primitive octave *e-e*, rather than an enlargement by the addition of tetrachords at both ends.

M. Gevaert regards the adaptation of the scheme to the other keys as the result of a gradual process of extension. Here we may distinguish between the recourse to the modified characters—which served essentially the same purpose as the 'sharps' and 'flats' in the signature of a modern key—and the additional notes obtained either by means of new characters ( ⌐ and Ɛ ), or by the use of accents ( ⌐' , &c.). The Hypo-dorian and Hypo-phrygian, which employ the new characters ⌐ and Ɛ , are known to be comparatively recent. The Phrygian and Lydian, it is true, employ the accented notes; but they do so only in the highest tetrachord (Hyperbolaiôn), which may not have been originally used in these high keys. The modified characters doubtless belong to an earlier period. They are needed for the three oldest keys—Dorian, Phrygian, Lydian—and also for the Enharmonic and Chromatic genera. If they are not part of the original scheme, the musician who devised them may fairly be counted as the second inventor of the instrumental notation.

In setting out the scales of the several keys it will be unnecessary to give more than the standing notes (**phthongoi hestôtes**), which are nearly all represented by original or unmodified letters—the moveable notes being represented by the modified forms described above. The following list includes the standing notes, viz. Proslambanomenos, Hypatê Hypatôn, Hypatê Mesôn, Mesê, Paramesê, Nêtê Diezeugmenôn and Nêtê Hyperbolaiôn in the seven oldest keys: the two lowest are marked as doubtful:—

| | Prosl. | Hyp. Hypatón. | Hyp. Mesôn. | Mesé. | Par. | Neté Diez. | Neté Hyperb. | |
|---|---|---|---|---|---|---|---|---|
| Mixo-lydian | ⊣ | И | Ɔ | > | N | ⅃ | | = e♭– e♭ |
| Lydian | Ⱶ | Γ | C | < | Ⅽ | Ⅵ | | = d – d |
| Phrygian | E | Ⱶ | F | Π | < | Z | | = c – c |
| Dorian | Ꞃ | E | И | Ɔ | Π | N | ⅃ | = b♭– b♭ |
| Hypo-lydian | H | h | Γ | C | K | Ⅽ | Ⅵ | = a – a |
| [Hypo-phrygian | | H | Ⱶ | F | C | < | Z | = g – g] |
| [Hypo-dorian | | | E | И | F | Π | N | = f – f] |

It will be evident that this scheme of notation tallies fairly well with what we know of the compass of Greek instruments about the end of the fifth century, and also with the account which Aristoxenus gives of the keys in use up to his time. We need only refer to what has been said above on p. 17 and p. 37.

It would be beyond the scope of this essay to discuss the date of the Greek musical notation. A few remarks, however, may be made, especially with reference to the high antiquity assigned to it by Westphal.

The alphabet from which it was derived was certainly an archaic one. It contained several characters, in particular $F$ for digamma, $Ꞁ$ for iota, and $Λ$ for lambda, which belong to the period before the introduction of the Ionian alphabet. Indeed if we were to judge from these letters alone we should be led to assign the instrumental notation (as Westphal does) to the time of Solon. The three-stroke iota ( $Ꞁ$ ), in particular, does not occur in any alphabet later than the sixth century B.C. On the other hand, when we find that the notation implies the use of a musical System in advance of any scale recognised in Aristotle, or even in Aristoxenus, such a date becomes incredible. We can only suppose either (1) that the use of $Ꞁ$ in the fifth century was confined to localities of which we have no complete epigraphic record, or (2) that $Ꞁ$ as a form of iota was still known—as archaic forms must have been—from the older public inscriptions, and was adopted by the inventor of the notation as being better suited to his purpose than $Ɩ$.

With regard to the place of origin of the notation the chief fact which we have to deal with is the use of the character $Ⱶ$ for lambda, which is distinctive of the alphabet of Argos, along with the commoner form $<$ .

Westphal indeed asserts that both these forms are found in the Argive alphabet. But the inscription (**C. I. 1**) which he quotes [27] for ⋖ really contains only ⊢ in a slightly different form. We cannot therefore say that the inventor of the notation derived it entirely from the alphabet of Argos, but only that he shows an acquaintance with that alphabet. This is confirmed by the fact that the form ⌐ for iota is not found at Argos. Probably therefore the inventor drew upon more than one alphabet for his purpose, the Argive alphabet being one.

The special fitness of the notation for the scales of the Enharmonic genus may be regarded as a further indication of its date. We shall see presently that that genus held a peculiar predominance in the earliest period of musical theory—that, namely, which was brought to an end by Aristoxenus.

If the author of the notation—or the second author, inventor of the modified characters—was one of the musicians whose names have come down to us, it would be difficult to find a more probable one than that of Pronomus of Thebes. One of the most striking features of the notation, at the time when it was framed, must have been the adjustment of the keys. Even in the time of Aristoxenus, as we know from the passage so often quoted, that adjustment was not universal. But it is precisely what Pronomus of Thebes is said to have done for the music of the flute (*supra*, p. 38). The circumstance that the system was only used for instrumental music is at least in harmony with this conjecture. If it is thought that Thebes is too far from Argos, we may fall back upon the notice that Sacadas of Argos was the chief composer for the flute before the time of Pronomus, [28] and doubtless Argos was one of the first cities to share in the advance which Pronomus made in the technique of his art.

# § 28. Traces of the Species in the Notation.

Before leaving this part of the subject it will be well to notice the attempt which Westphal makes to connect the species of the Octave with the form of the musical notation.

The basis of the notation, as has been explained (p. 69), is formed by two Diatonic octaves, denoted by the letters of the alphabet from α to ν, as follows:

η ι ε λ γ μ F θ κ δ λ β ν ζ α

*a b c d e f g a b c d e f g a*

In this scale, as has been pointed out (p. 71), the notes which are at the distance of an octave from each other are always expressed by two *successive* letters of the alphabet. Thus we find—

β - γ  is the octave  *e - e,*  the Dorian species.

δ - ε  " "  *c - c,*  the Lydian species.

F - ζ  " "  *g - g,*  the Hypo-phrygian species.

η - θ  " "  *a - a,*  the Hypo-dorian species.

Westphal adopts the theory of Boeckh (as to which see p. 11) that the Hypo-phrygian and Hypo-dorian species answered to the ancient Ionian and Aeolian modes. On this assumption he argues that the order of the pairs of letters representing the species agrees with the order of the Modes in the historical development of Greek music. For the priority of Dorian, Ionian, and Aeolian he appeals to the authority of Heraclides Ponticus, quoted above (p. 9). The Lydian, he supposes, was interposed in the second place on account of its importance in education,—recognised, as we have seen, by Aristotle in the *Politics* (viii. 7 *ad fin.*). Hence he regards the notation as confirming his theory of the nature and history of the Modes.

The weakness of this reasoning is manifold. Granting that the Hypo-dorian and Hypo-phrygian answer to the old Aeolian and Ionian respectively, we have to ask what is the nature of the priority which Heraclides Ponticus claims for his three modes, and what is the value of his testimony. What he says is, in substance, that these are the only kinds of music that are truly Hellenic, and worthy of the name of modes (**harmoniai**). It can hardly be thought that this is a criticism likely to have weighed with the inventor of the notation. But if it did, why did he give an equally prominent place to Lydian, one of the modes which Heraclides condemned? In fact, the introduction of Lydian goes far to show that the coincidence—such as it is—with the views of Heraclides is mere accident. Apart, however, from these difficulties, there are at least two considerations which seem fatal to Westphal's theory:

1. The notation, so far as the original two octaves are concerned, must have been devised and worked out at some one time. No part of these two octaves can have been completed before the rest. Hence the order in which the letters are taken for the several notes has no historical importance.

2. The notation does not represent only the *species* of a scale, that is to say, the relative pitch of the notes which compose it, but it represents also the absolute pitch of each note. Thus the octaves which are defined by the successive pairs of letters, β-γ, δ-ε, and the rest, are octaves of definite notes. If they were framed with a view to the ancient modes, as Westphal thinks, they must be the actual scales employed in these modes. If so, the modes followed each other, in respect of pitch, in an order exactly the reverse of the order observed in the keys. It need hardly be said that this is quite impossible.

# § 29. Ptolemy's Scheme of Modes.

The first writer who takes the Species of the Octave as the basis of the musical scales is the mathematician Claudius Ptolemaeus (fl. 140-160 A.D.). In his *Harmonics* he virtually sets aside the scheme of keys elaborated by Aristoxenus and his school, and adopts in their place a system of scales answering in their main features to the mediaeval Tones or Modes. The object of difference of key, he says, is not that the music as a whole may be of a higher or lower pitch, but that a melody may be brought within a certain compass. For this purpose it is necessary to vary the succession of intervals (as a modern musician does by changing the signature of the clef). If, for example, we take the Perfect System (**systêma ametabolon**) in the key of *a* minor—which is its natural key,—and transpose it to the key of *d* minor, we do so, according to Ptolemy, not in order to raise the general pitch of our music by a Fourth, but because we wish to have a scale with *b* flat instead of *b* natural. The flattening of this note, however, means that the two octaves change their species. They are now of the species *e-e*. Thus, instead of transposing the Perfect System into different keys, we arrive more directly at the desired result by changing the species of its octaves. And as there are seven possible species of the Octave, we obtain seven different Systems or scales. From these assumptions it follows, as Ptolemy shows in some detail, that any greater number of keys is useless. If a key is an octave higher than another, it is superfluous because it gives us a mere repetition of the same intervals [29].

If we interpose a key between (*e.g.*) the Hypo-dorian and the Hypo-phrygian, it must give us over again either the Hypo-dorian or the Hypo-phrygian scale [30]. Thus the fifteen keys of the Aristoxeneans are reduced to seven, and these seven are not transpositions of a single scale, but are all of the same pitch. See the table at the end of the book.

With this scheme of Keys Ptolemy combined a new method of naming the individual notes. The old method, by which a note was named from its relative place in the Perfect System, must evidently have become inconvenient. The Lydian Mesê, for example, was two tones higher than the Dorian Mesê, because the Lydian scale as a whole was two tones higher than the Dorian. But when the two scales were reduced to the same compass, the old Lydian Mesê was no longer in the middle of the scale, and the name ceased to have a meaning. It is as though the term 'dominant' when applied to a Minor key were made to mean the dominant of the relative Major key. On Ptolemy's method the notes of each scale were named from their places in it. The old names were used, Proslambanomenos for the lowest, Hypatê

Hypatôn for the next, and so on, but without regard to the intervals between the notes. Thus there were two methods of naming, that which had been in use hitherto, termed 'nomenclature according to *value*' (**onomasia kata dynamin**), and the new method of naming from the various scales, termed 'nomenclature according to *position*' (**onomasia kata thesin**). The former was in effect a retention of the Perfect System and the Keys: the latter put in their place a scheme of seven different standard Systems.

In illustration of his theory Ptolemy gives tables showing in numbers the intervals of the octaves used in the different keys and genera. He shows two octaves in each key, viz. that from Hypatê Mesôn (**kata thesin**) to Nêtê Diezeugmenôn (called the octave **apo nêtês**), and that from Proslambanomenos to Mesê (the octave **apo mesês**). As he also gives the divisions of five different 'colours' or varieties of genus, the whole number of octaves is no less than seventy.

Ptolemy does not exclude difference of pitch altogether. The whole instrument, he says, may be tuned higher or lower at pleasure [31]. Thus the pitch is treated by him as modern notation treats the *tempo*, viz. as something which is not absolutely given, but has to be supplied by the individual performer.

Although the language of Ptolemy's exposition is studiously impersonal, it may be gathered that his reduction of the number of keys from fifteen to seven was an innovation proposed by himself [32]. If this is so, the rest of the scheme,—the elimination of the element of pitch, and the 'nomenclature by position,'—must also be due to him. Here, however, we find ourselves at issue with Westphal and those who agree with him on the main question of the Modes. According to Westphal the nomenclature by position is mentioned by Aristoxenus, and is implied in at least one important passage of the Aristotelian *Problems*. We have now to examine the evidence which he adduces to support his contention.

# § 30. Nomenclature by Position.

Two passages of Aristoxenus are quoted by Westphal in support of his contention. The first (p. 6 Meib.) is one in which Aristoxenus announces his intention to treat of Systems, their number and nature: 'setting out their differences in respect of compass (**megethos**), and for each compass the differences in form and composition and position (**tas te kata schêma kai kata synthesin kai kata thesin**), so that no element of melody,—either compass or form or composition or position,—may be unexplained.' But the word **thesis**, when applied to Systems, does not mean the 'position' of single notes, but of groups of notes. Elsewhere (p. 54 Meib.) he speaks of the position of tetrachords towards each other (**tas tôn tetrachordôn pros allêla theseis**), laying it down that any two tetrachords in the same System must be consonant either with each other or with some third tetrachord. The other passage quoted by Westphal (p. 69 Meib.) is also in the discussion of Systems. Aristoxenus is pointing out the necessity of recognising that some elements of melodious succession are fixed and limited, others are unlimited:

> **kata men oun ta megethê tôn diastêmatôn kai tas tôn phthongôn taseis apeira pôs phainetai einai ta peri melos, kata de tas dynameis kai kata ta eidê kai kata tas theseis peperasmena te kai tetagmena.**

> 'In the size of the intervals and the pitch of the notes the elements of melody seem to be infinite; but in respect of the values (*i.e.* the relative places of the notes) and in respect of the forms (*i.e.* the succession of the intervals) and in respect of the positions they are limited and settled.'

Aristoxenus goes on to illustrate this by supposing that we wish to continue a scale downwards from a **pyknon** or pair of small intervals (Chromatic or Enharmonic). In this case, as the **pyknon** forms the lower part of a tetrachord, there are two possibilities. If the next lower tetrachord is disjunct, the next interval is a tone; if it is conjunct, the next interval is the large interval of the genus (**hê men gar kata tonon eis diazeuxin agei to tou systêmatos eidos, hê de kata thateron diastêma ho ti dêpot' echei megethos eis synaphên**). Thus the succession of intervals is determined by the relative position of the two tetrachords, as to which there is a choice between two definite alternatives. This then is evidently what is meant by the words **kata tas theseis** [33]. On the other hand the **thesis** of Ptolemy's nomenclature is the absolute pitch (*Harm.* ii. 5 **pote men par' autên tên thesin, to oxyteron haplôs ê baryteron, onomazomen**), and this is one of the elements which according to Aristoxenus are indefinite.

Westphal also finds the nomenclature by position implied in the passage of the Aristotelian *Problems* (xix. 20) which deals with the peculiar relation of the Mesê to the rest of the musical scale. The passage has already been quoted and discussed (*supra*, p. 43), and it has been pointed out that if the Mesê of the Perfect System (**mesê kata dynamin**) is the key-note, the scale must have been an octave of the *a*-species. If octaves of other species were used, as Westphal maintains, it becomes necessary to take the Mesê of this passage to be the **mesê kata thesin**, or Mesê by position. That is, Westphal is obliged by his theory of the Modes to take the term Mesê in a sense of which there is no other trace before the time of Ptolemy. But—

(1) It is highly improbable that the names of the notes—Mesê, Hypatê, Nêtê and the rest—should have had two distinct meanings. Such an ambiguity would have been intolerable, and only to be compared with the similar ambiguity which Westphal's theory implies in the use of the terms Dorian, &c.

(2) If the different species of the octave were the practically important scales, as Westphal maintains, the position of the notes in these scales must have been correspondingly important. Hence the nomenclature by position must have been the more usual and familiar one. Yet, as we have shown, it is not found in Aristotle, Aristoxenus or Euclid—to say nothing of later writers.

(3) The nomenclature by position is an essential part of the scheme of Keys proposed by Ptolemy. It bears the same relation to Ptolemy's octaves as the nomenclature by 'value' bears to the old standard octave and the Perfect System. It was probably therefore devised about the time of Ptolemy, if not actually by him.

# § 31. Scales of the Lyre and Cithara.

The earliest evidence in practical music of any octaves other than those of the standard System is to be found in the account given by Ptolemy of certain scales employed on the lyre and cithara. According to this account the scales of the lyre (the simpler and commoner instrument) were of two kinds. One was Diatonic, of the 'colour' or variety which Ptolemy recognises as the prevailing one, viz. the 'Middle Soft' or 'Tonic' (**diatonon toniaion**) [34]. The other was a 'mixture' of this Diatonic with the standard Chromatic (**chrôma suntonon**): that is to say, the octave consisted of a tetrachord of each genus. These octaves apparently might be of any *species*, according to the key chosen [35]. On the cithara,—which was a more elaborate form of lyre, confined in practice to professional musicians,—six different octave scales were employed, each of a particular species and key. They are enumerated and described by Ptolemy in two passages (*Harm.* i. 16 and ii. 16), which in some points serve to correct each other [36]. Of the six scales two are of the Hypodorian or Common species (*a-a*). One of these, called **tritai**, is purely Diatonic of the Middle Soft variety; the intervals expressed by fractions are as follows:

$a$ 9/8 $b$ 28/27 $c$ 8/7 $d$ 9/8 $e$ 28/27 $f$ 8/7 $g$ 9/8 $a$

The other, called **tropoi** or **tropika**, is a mixture, Middle Soft Diatonic in the upper tetrachord, and Chromatic in the lower:

$a$ 9/8 $b$ 22/21 $c$ 12/11 $\sharp$ 7/6 $e$ 28/27 $f$ 8/7 $g$ 9/8 $a$

Two scales are of the Dorian or *e*-species, viz. **parypatai**, a combination of Soft and Middle Soft Diatonic:

$e$ 21/20 $f$ 10/9 $g$ 8/7 $a$ 9/8 $b$ 28/27 $c$ 8/7 $d$ 9/8 $e$

and **lydia**, in which the upper tetrachord is of the strict or 'highly strung' Diatonic (**diatonon syntonon**—our 'natural' temperament):

$e$ 28/27 $f$ 8/7 $g$ 9/8 $a$ 9/8 $b$ 16/15 $c$ 9/8 $d$ 10/9 $e$

> Westphal (*Harmonik und Melopöie*, 1863, p. 255) supposes a much deeper corruption. He would restore **ta de lydia [kai iastia hoi tou migmatos tou syntonou diatonou tou ... ta de ...] hoi tou toniaiou diatonou tou Dôriou**. This introduces a serious discrepancy between the two passages, as the number of scales in the second list is raised to eight (Westphal making **iastia** and **iastiaioliaia** distinct scales, and furthermore inserting a new scale, of unknown name).

Moreover the (unknown) scale of unmixed **diatonon toniaion** is out of its place at the end of the list. Westphal's objection to **lydia** as the name of a scale of the *Dorian* species of course only holds good on his theory of the Modes.

The only other differences between the two passages are:

(1) In the scales of the lyre called **malaka** the admixture, according to i. 16, is one of **chrômatikon syntonon**, according to ii. 16 of **chr. malakon**. But, as Westphal shows, Soft Chromatic is not admitted by Ptolemy as in practical use. It would seem that in the second passage the copyist was led astray by the word **malaka** just before.

(2) The **iastia** of i. 16 is called **astiaioliaia** in ii. 16. We need not suppose the text to be faulty, since the two forms may have been both in use.

Another point overlooked in Westphal's treatment is that **diatonon syntonon** and **d. ditoniaion** are not really distinguished by Ptolemy. In one passage (i. 16) he gives his **lydia** and **iastia** as a mixture with **d. syntonon**, adding that in practice it was **d. ditoniaion**. In the other (ii. 16) he speaks at once of **d. ditoniaion**. This consideration brings the two places into such close agreement that any hypothesis involving discrepancy is most improbable.

In practice it appears that musicians tuned the tetrachord *b-e* of this scale with the Pythagorean two Major tones and **leimma**.

Of the remaining scales one, called **hypertropa**, is Phrygian in species (*d-d*), and of the standard genus:

*d* 9/8  *e* 28/27  *f* 8/7  *g* 9/8  *a* 9/8  *b* 28/27  *c* 8/7  *d*

One, called **iastia**, or **iastiaioliaia**, is of the Hypo-phrygian or *g*-species, the tetrachord *b-e* being 'highly strung' Diatonic or (in practice) Pythagorean, viz.:

*g* 9/8  *a* 9/8  *b* 256/243  *c* 9/8  *d* 9/8  *e* 28/27  *f* 8/7  *g*

Regarding the tonality of these scales there is not very much to be said. In the case of the Hypo-dorian and Dorian octaves it will be generally thought probable that the key-note is *a* (the **mesê kata dynamin**). If so, the difference between the two species is not one of 'mode,'—in the modern sense,—but consists in the fact that in the Hypo-dorian the compass of the melody is from the key-note upwards, while in the Dorian it extends a Fourth below the key-note. It is possible, however, that the lowest note (*e*) of the Dorian octave was sometimes the key-note: in which case the *mode* was properly Dorian. In the Phrygian octave of Ptolemy's description the key-note cannot be the Fourth or Mesê **kata thesin** (*g*), since the interval *g-c* is not consonant (9/8 × 9/8 × 28/27 being less than 4/3). Possibly the lowest note (*d*) is the key-note; if so the scale is of the Phrygian mode (in the modern sense). In the Hypo-phrygian octave there is a similar objection to regarding the Mesê **kata thesin** (*c*) as the key-note, and some probability in favour of the lowest note (*g*). If the Pythagorean division of the tetrachord *g-c* were replaced by the natural temperament, which the language used by Ptolemy [37] leads us to regard as the true division, the scale would exhibit the intervals—

*g* 5/4   *b* 6/5   *d* 7/6   *f* 8/7   *g*

which give the natural chord of the Seventh. This however is no more than a hypothesis.

It evidently follows from all this that Ptolemy's octaves do not constitute a system of *modes*. They are merely the groups of notes, of the compass of an octave, which are most likely to be used in the several keys, and which Ptolemy or some earlier theorist chose to call by the names of those keys.

# § 32. Remains of Greek Music.

The extant specimens of Greek music are mostly of the second century A.D., and therefore nearly contemporary with Ptolemy. The most considerable are the melodies of three lyrical pieces or hymns, viz. (1) a hymn to Calliope, (2) a hymn to Apollo (or Helios),—both ascribed to a certain Dionysius,—and (3) a hymn to Nemesis, ascribed to Mesomedes [38]. Besides these there are (4) some short instrumental passages or exercises given by Bellermann's *Anonymus* (pp. 94-96). And quite recently the list has been increased by (5) an inscription discovered by Mr. W. M. Ramsay, which gives a musical setting of four short gnomic sentences, and (6) a papyrus fragment (now in the collection of the Arch-duke Rainer) of the music of a chorus in the *Orestes* of Euripides. These two last additions to our scanty stock of Greek music are set out and discussed by Dr. Wessely of Vienna and M. Ruelle in the *Revue des Études Grecques* (V. 1892, pp. 265-280), also by Dr. Otto Crusius in the *Philologus*, Vol. LII, pp. 160-200 [39].

The music of the three hymns is noted in the Lydian key (answering to the modern scale with one b). The melody of the second hymn is of the compass of an octave, the notes being those of the Perfect System from Parhypatê Hypatôn to Tritê Diezeugmenôn (*f-f* with one b). The first employs the same octave with a lower note added, viz. Hypatê Hypatôn (*e*): the third adds the next higher note, Paranêtê Diezeugmenôn (*g*). Thus the Lydian key may be said, in the case of the second hymn, and less exactly in the case of the two others, to give the Lydian or *c*-species of the octave in the most convenient part of the scale; just as on Ptolemy's system of Modes we should expect it to do.

This octave, however, represents merely the *compass* (*ambitus* or *tessitura*) of the melody: it has nothing to do with its *tonality*. In the first two hymns, as Bellermann pointed out, the key-note is the Hypatê Mesôn; and the mode— in the modern sense of that word—is that of the octave *e-e* (the Dorian mode of Helmholtz's theory). In the third hymn the key-note appears to be the Lichanos Mesôn, so that the mode is that of *g-g*, viz. the Hypo-phrygian.

Of the instrumental passages given by the *Anonymus* three are clearly in the Hypo-dorian or common mode, the Mesê (*a*) being the key-note. (See Gevaert, i. p. 141.) A fourth (§ 104) also ends on the Mesê, but the key-note appears to be the Parhypatê Mesôn (*f*). Accordingly Westphal and Gevaert assign it to the Hypo-lydian species (*f-f*). In Westphal's view the circumstance of the end of the melody falling, not on the key-note, but on the Third or Mediant of the octave, was characteristic of the Modes distinguished by the prefix *syntono-*, and accordingly the passage in question is pronounced by him to be Syntono-lydian. All those passages, however, are mere fragments of two or three bars each, and are quoted as examples of certain peculiarities of rhythm. They can hardly be made to lend much support to any theory of the Modes.

The music of Mr. Ramsay's inscription labours under the same defect of excessive shortness. If, however, we regard the four brief sentences as set to a continuous melody, we obtain a passage consisting of thirty-six notes in all, with a compass of less than an octave, and ending on the lowest note of that compass. Unlike the other extant specimens of Greek music it is written in the Ionian key—a curious fact which has not been noticed by Dr. Wessely.

INSCRIPTION WITH MUSICAL NOTES.

ὅσ - ον ζῇς φαί - - νου.

μη - δὲν ὅλ - ως σὺ λυ - ποῦ.

πρὸς ὀ - λί - γον ἐσ - τὶ τὸ ζῆν.

τὸ τέ - λος ὁ χρό - νος ἀ - παι - τεῖ.

hos-on zês phai-nou.
mê-den hol-ôs sy ly-pou.
pros o-li-gon es-ti to zên.
to te-los ho chro-nos a-pai-tei.

The notes which enter into this melody form the scale *f#-g-a-b-c#-d-e-f#*, which is an octave of the Dorian species (*e-e* on the white notes). Hence if *f#*, on which the melody ends, is the key-note, the *mode* is the Dorian. On the other hand the predominant notes are those of the triad *a-c#-e*, which point to the key of *a* major, with the difference that the Seventh is flat (*g* instead of *g♯*). On this view the music would be in the Hypo-phrygian mode.

However this may be, the most singular feature of this fragment remains to be mentioned, viz. the agreement between the musical notes and the *accentuation* of the words. We know from the grammarians that an acute accent signified that the vowel was sounded with a rise in the pitch of the voice, and that a circumflex denoted a rise followed on the same syllable by a lower note—every such rise and fall being quite independent both of syllabic quantity and of stress or *ictus*. Thus in ordinary speech the accents formed a species of melody,—**logôdes ti melos**, as it is called by Aristoxenus [40]. When words were *sung* this 'spoken melody' was no longer heard, being superseded by the melody proper. Dionysius of Halicarnassus is at pains to explain (*De Comp. Verb.*, c. 11), that the melody to which words are set does not usually follow or resemble the quasi-melody of the accents, *e.g.* in the following words of a chorus in the *Orestes* of Euripides (ll. 140-142):—

**siga siga leukon ichnos arbylês**
**tithete, mê ktypeite;**
**apoprobat' ekeis' apopro moi koitas,**

he notices that the melody differs in several points from the spoken accents: (1) the three first words are all on the same note, in spite of the accents; (2) the last syllable of **arbylês** is as high as the second, though that is the only accented syllable: (3) the first syllable of **tithete** is lower than the two others, instead of being higher: (4) the circumflex of **ktypeite** is lost (**êphanistai**), because the word is all on the same pitch; (5) the fourth syllable of **apoprobate** is higher in pitch, instead of the third. In Mr. Ramsay's inscription, however, the music follows the accents as closely as possible. Every acute accent coincides with a rise of pitch, except in **hoson**, which begins the melody, and in **esti**, for which we should perhaps read the orthotone **esti**. Of the four instances of the circumflex accent three exhibit the two notes and the falling pitch which we expect. The interval is either a major or a minor Third. In the other case (**zês**) the next note is a Third lower: but it does not seem to belong to the circumflexed syllable. All this cannot be accidental. It leads us to the conclusion that the musical notes represent a kind of recitative, or imitation of spoken words, rather than a melody in the proper sense of the term.

If any considerable specimen of the music of Euripides had survived, it might have solved many of the problems with which we have been dealing. The fragment before us extends over about six lines in dochmiac metre (*Orestes*

338-343), with the vocal notation: but no single line is entire. The key is the Lydian. The genus is either Enharmonic or Chromatic. Assuming that it is Enharmonic—the alternative adopted by Dr. Wessely—the characters which are still legible may be represented in modern notation as follows:

[EURIPIDES, *Orestes* 338-344.

(κατολο)φύ - ρο - μαι·   μα - τέ - ρος (αἶμα σᾶς ὅ σ' ἀνα)βακ - χεύ - ει·

ὁ   μέ - γας (ὄλβος οὐ μόνιμο)ς ἐν   βρο - τοῖς·

ἀ - νὰ (δὲ λαῖφος ὥς τι)ς ἀ - κά - του   θο - ᾶς   τι - νά(ξας δαίμων)

κατ) - έ - κλυ - σεν (δεινῶν πόνων) ὡς   πόν - (του λαβροῖς κ.τ.λ.

?   ?   ?

(katolo)phy-ro-mai; ma-te-ros (haima sas ho d' ana)bak-cheu-ei;
ho me-gas (olbos ou monimo)s en bro-tois;
a-na (de laiphos hôs ti)s a-ka-tou tho-as ti-na(xas daimôn)
kat-e-kly-sen (deinôn ponon) hôs pon-tou labrois   k.t.l.

It should be observed that in the fragment the line **katolophyromai katolophyromai** comes before 338 (**materos k.t.l.**), not after it, as in our texts [41].

The notes employed, according to the interpretation given above, give the scale *g-a-a\*-a♯-d-e-e\**. If the genus is Chromatic, as M. Ruelle is disposed to think, they are *g-a-a♯-b-d-e-f*. When these scales are compared with the Perfect System we find that they do not entirely agree with it. Whether the genus is Enharmonic or Chromatic the notes from *a* to *e\** (or *f*) answer to those of the Perfect System (of the same genus) from Hypatê Mesôn to Tritê

- 72 -

Diezeugmenôn. But in either case the lowest note ($g$) finds no place in the System, since it can only be the Diatonic Lichanos Hypatôn. It is possible, however, that the scale belongs to the period when the original octave had been extended by the addition of a tone below the Hypatê—the note, in fact, which we have already met with under the name of Hyper-hypatê (p. 39). Thus the complete scale may have consisted of the disjunct tetrachords *a-d* and *e-a*, with the tone *g-a*. It may be observed here that although the scale in question does not fit into the Perfect System, it conforms to the general rules laid down by Aristoxenus for the melodious succession of intervals. It is unnecessary therefore to suppose (as Dr. Wessely and M. Ruelle do) that the scale exhibits a *mixture* of different genera.

It must be vain to attempt to discover the tonality of a short fragment which has neither beginning nor end. The only group of notes which has the character of a cadence is that on the word **(olo)phypomai**, and again on the words **en brotois**, viz. the notes *a♯ a\* a* (if the genus is the Enharmonic). The same notes occur in reversed order on **akatou** and **(kat)eklusen**. This seems to bear out the common view of the Enharmonic as produced by the introduction of an 'accidental' or passing note. It will be seen, in fact, that the Enharmonic notes (*a\** and *e\**) only occur before or after the 'standing' notes (*a* and *e*).

Relying on the fact that the lowest note is *g*, Dr. Wessely and M. Ruelle pronounce the mode to be the Phrygian (*g-g* in the key with one ♭, or *d-d* in the natural key). I have already put forward a different explanation of this *g*, and will only add here that it occurs twice in the fragment, both times on a short syllable [42]. The important notes, so far as the evidence goes, are *a*, which twice comes at the end of a verse (with a pause in the sense), and *e*, which once has that position. If *a* is the key-note, the mode—in the modern sense—is Dorian (the *e*-species). If *e* is the key-note, it is Mixo-lydian (the ♭-species).

# § 33. Modes of Aristides Quintilianus.

The most direct testimony in support of the view that the ancient Modes were differentiated by the succession of their intervals has still to be considered. It is the account given by Aristides Quintilianus (p. 21 Meib.) of the six Modes (**harmoniai**) of Plato's *Republic*. After describing the genera and their varieties the 'colours,' he goes on to say that there were other divisions of the tetrachord (**tetrachordikai diaireseis**) which the most ancient musicians used for the **harmoniai**, and that these were sometimes greater in compass than the octave, sometimes less. He then gives the intervals of the scale for each of the six Modes mentioned by Plato, and adds the scales in the ancient notation. They are of the Enharmonic genus, and may be represented by modern notes as follows:—

| | |
|---|---|
| Mixo-lydian | *b-b\*-c-d-e-e\*-f-b* |
| Syntono-lydian | *e-e\*-f-a-c* |
| Phrygian | *d-e-e\*-f-a-b-b\*-c-d* |
| Dorian | *d-e-e\*-f-a-b-b\*-c-e* |
| Lydian | *e\*-f-a-b-b\*-c-e-e\** |
| Ionian | *e-e\*-f-a-c-d* |

Comparing these scales with the Species of the Octave, we find a certain amount of correspondence. As has been already noticed (p. 22), the names Syntono-lydian and Lydian answer to the ordinary Lydian and Hypo-lydian respectively. Accordingly the Lydian of Aristides agrees with the Hypo-lydian species as given in the pseudo-Euclidean *Introductio*. The Dorian of Aristides is the Dorian species of the *Introductio*, but with an additional note, a tone below the Hypatê.

The Phrygian of Aristides is not the Enharmonic Phrygian species; but it is derived from the diatonic Phrygian octave *d-e-f-g-a-b-c-d* by inserting the enharmonic notes *e\** and *b\**, and omitting the diatonic *g*. By a similar process the Mixo-lydian of Aristides may be derived from the diatonic octave *b-b*, except that *a* as well as *g* is omitted, and on the other hand *d* is retained. If the scale of the Syntono-lydian is completed by the lower *c* (as analogy would require), it will answer similarly to the Lydian species (*c-c*).

# § 34. Credibility of Aristides Quintilianus.

But what weight can be given to Aristides as an authority on the music of the time of Plato? The answer to this question depends upon several considerations.

1. The date of Aristides is unknown. He is certainly later than Cicero, since he quotes the *De Republica* (p. 70 Meib.). From the circumstance that he makes no reference to the musical innovations of Ptolemy it has been supposed that he was earlier than that writer. But, as Aristides usually confines himself to the theory of Aristoxenus and his school, the argument from silence is not of much value. On the other hand he gives a scheme of notation containing two characters, Ɫ and ✱, which extend the scale two successive semi-tones beyond the lowest point of the notation given by Alypius [43]. For this reason it is probable that Aristides is one of the latest of the writers on ancient music.

2. The manner in which Aristides introduces his information about the Platonic Modes is highly suspicious. He has been describing the various divisions of the tetrachord according to the theory of Aristoxenus, and adds that there were anciently other divisions in use. So far Aristides is doubtless right, since Aristoxenus himself says that the divisions of the tetrachord are theoretically infinite in number (p. 26 Meib.),—that it is possible, for example, to combine the Parhypatê of the Soft Chromatic with the Lichanos of the Diatonic (p. 52 Meib.). But all this concerns the genus of the scale, and has nothing to do with the species of the Octave, with which Aristides proceeds to connect it. It follows either that there is some confusion in the text, or that Aristides was compiling from sources which he did not understand.

3. The Platonic Modes were a subject of interest to the early musical writers, and were discussed by Aristoxenus himself (Plut. *de Mus.* c. 17). If Aristoxenus had had access to such an account as we have in Aristides, we must have found some trace of it, either in the extant *Harmonics* or in the quotations of Plutarch and other compilers.

4. Of the four scales which extend to the compass of an octave, only one, viz. the Dorian, conforms to the rules which are said by Aristoxenus to have prevailed in early Greek music. The Phrygian divides the Fourth *a-d* into four intervals instead of three, by the sequence *a b b\* c d*. As has been observed, it is neither the Enharmonic Phrygian species (*c e e\* f a b b\* c*), nor the Diatonic *d-d*, but a mixture of the two. Similarly the Mixo-lydian divides the Fourth *b-e* into four intervals (*b b\* c d e*), by introducing the purely Diatonic

note *d*. The Lydian is certainly the Lydian Enharmonic species of the pseudo-Euclid; but we can hardly suppose that it existed in practical music. Aristoxenus lays it down emphatically that a quarter-tone is always followed by another: and we cannot imagine a scale in which the highest and lowest notes are in no harmonic relation to the rest.

5. Two of the scales are incomplete, viz. the Ionian, which has six notes and the compass of a Seventh, and the Syntono-lydian, which consists of five notes, with the compass of a Minor Sixth. We naturally look for parallels among the defective scales noticed in the *Problems* and in Plutarch's dialogues. But we find little that even illustrates the modes of Aristides. The scales noticed in the *Problems* (xix. 7, 32, 47) are hepta-chord, and generally of the compass of an octave. In one passage of Plutarch (*De Mus.* c. 11) there is a description—quoted from Aristoxenus—of an older kind of Enharmonic, in which the semitones had not yet been divided into quarter-tones. In another chapter (c. 19) he speaks of the omission of the Tritê and also of the Nêtê as characteristic of a form of music called the **spondeiakos tropos**. It may be said that in the Ionian and Syntono-lydian of Aristides the Enharmonic Tritê (*b\**) and the Nêtê (*e*) are wanting. But the Paramesê (*b*) is also wanting in both these modes. And the Ionian is open to the observation already made with regard to the Phrygian, viz. that the two highest notes (*c d*) involve a mixture of Diatonic with Enharmonic scale. We may add that Plutarch (who evidently wrote with Aristoxenus before him) gives no hint that the omission of these notes was characteristic of any particular modes.

6. It is impossible to decide the question of the modes of Aristides without some reference to another statement of the same author. In the chapter which treats of Intervals (pp. 13-15 Meib.) he gives the ancient division of two octaves, the first into dieses or quarter-tones, the second into semitones. The former of these (**hê para tois archaiois kata dieseis harmonia**) is as follows:

| [1] | 2 | 3 | 4 | 5 | 6 | 7 | 8 | 9 | 10 | 11 | 12 |
|-----|---|---|---|---|---|---|---|---|----|----|----|
| | -o | < | 6 | ⊔ | ϙ | L | ⌐ | Δ | ∇ | Є | Ɔ |
| | o- | > | 9 | ⊓ | ♭ | ⌐ | Γ | ∇ | Δ | Ɔ | Є |

| 13 | 14 | 15 | 16 | 17 | 18 | 19 | 20 | 21 | 22 | 23 | 24 |
|----|----|----|----|----|----|----|----|----|----|----|----|
| ⊐ | Γ | Ч | Ɔ | Є | �卜 | ⅃ | ∝ | > | < | Y | Y |
| Γ | ⊐ | Ħ | Є | Ɔ | ⅄ | ⊦ | ∞ | < | > | Y | Y |

After every allowance has been made for the probability that these signs or some of them have reached us in a corrupt form, it is impossible to reduce them to the ordinary notation, as Meibomius sought to do. The scholar who first published them as they stand in the MSS. (F. L. Perne, see Bellermann, *Tonleitern*, p. 62) regarded them as a relic of a much older system of notation. This is in accordance with the language of Aristides, and indeed is the only view consistent with a belief in their genuineness. They are too like the ordinary notation to be quite independent, and cannot have been put forward as an improvement upon it. Are they, then, earlier? Bellermann has called our attention to a peculiarity which seems fatal to any such claim. They consist, like the ordinary signs, of two sets, one written above the other, and in every instance one of the pair is simply a reversed or inverted form of the other. With the ordinary signs this is not generally the case, since the two sets, the vocal and instrumental notes, are originally independent. But it is the case with the three lowest notes, viz. those which were added to the series at a later time. When these additional signs were invented the vocal and instrumental notes had come to be employed together. The inventor therefore devised a pair of signs in each case, and not unnaturally made them correspond in form. In the scale given by Aristides this correspondence runs through the whole series, which must therefore be of later date. But if this is so, the characters can hardly represent a genuine system of notation. In other words, Aristides must have been imposed upon by a species of forgery.

7. Does the fragment of the *Orestes* tell for or against the Modes described by Aristides?

The scale which is formed by the notes of the fragment agrees, so far as it extends, with two of the scales now in question, viz. the Phrygian and the Dorian. Taking the view of its tonality expressed in the last chapter (p. 93), we should describe it as the Dorian scale of Aristides with the two highest notes omitted. The omission, in so short a fragment, is of little weight; and the agreement in the use of an additional lower note (Hyper-hypatê) is certainly worth notice. On the other hand, the Dorian is precisely the mode, of those given in the list of Aristides, which least needs defence, as it is the most faithful copy of the Perfect System. Hence the fact that it is verified by an actual piece of music does not go far in support of the other scales in the same list.

If our suspicions are well-founded, it is evident that they seriously affect the genuineness of all the antiquarian learning which Aristides sets before his readers, and in particular of his account of the Platonic modes. I venture to think that they go far to deprive that account of the value which it has been supposed to have for the history of the earliest Greek music.

For the later period, however, to which Aristides himself belongs, these apocryphal scales are a document of some importance. The fact that they do not agree entirely with the species of the Octave as given by the pseudo-Euclid leads us to think that they may be influenced by scales used in actual music. This applies especially to the Phrygian, which (as has been shown) is really diatonic. The Ionian, again, is perhaps merely an imperfect form of the same scale, viz. the octave *d-d* with lower *d* omitted. And the Syntono-lydian may be the Lydian diatonic octave *c-c* with a similar omission of the lower *c*.

# § 35. Evidence for Scales of different species.

The object of the foregoing discussion has been to show, in the first place, that there was no such distinction in ancient Greek music as that which scholars have drawn between Modes (**harmoniai**) and Keys (**tonoi** or **tropoi**): and, in the second place, that the musical scales denoted by these terms were primarily distinguished by difference of *pitch*,—that in fact they were so many keys of the standard scale known in its final form as the Perfect System. The evidence now brought forward in support of these two propositions is surely as complete as that which has been allowed to determine any question of ancient learning.

It does not, however, follow that the Greeks knew of no musical forms analogous to our Major and Minor modes, or to the mediaeval Tones. On the contrary, the course of the discussion has led us to recognise distinctions of this kind in more than one instance. The doctrine against which the argument has been mainly directed is not that ancient scales were of more than one species or 'mode' (as it is now called), but that difference of species was the basis of the ancient Greek Modes. This will become clear if we bring together all the indications which we have observed of scales differing from each other in species, that is, in the *order* of the intervals in the octave. In doing so it will be especially important to be guided by the principle which we laid down at the outset, of arranging our materials according to chronology, and judging of each piece of evidence strictly with reference to the period to which it belongs. It is only thus that we can hope to gain a conception of Greek music as the living and changing thing that we know it must have been.

1. The principal scale of Greek music is undoubtedly of the Hypo-dorian or common species. This is sufficiently proved by the facts (1) that two octaves of this species (*a-a*) constitute the scale known as the Greater Perfect System, and (2) that the central *a* of this system, called the Mesê, is said to have been the key-note, or at least to have had the kind of importance in the scale which we connect with the key-note (Arist. *Probl.* xix. 20). This mode, it is obvious, is based on the scale which is the descending scale of the modern Minor mode. It may therefore be identified with the Minor, except that it does not admit the leading note.

It should be observed that this mode is to be recognised not merely in the Perfect System but equally in the primitive octave, of the form *e-e*, out of which the Perfect System grew. The important point is the tonic character of the Mesê (*a*), and this, as it happens, rests upon the testimony of an author who knows the primitive octave only. The fact that that octave is of the so-called Dorian species does not alter the *mode* (as we are now using that term), but only the compass of the notes employed.

The Hypo-dorian octave is seen in two of the scales of the cithara given by Ptolemy (p. 85), viz. those called **tritai** and **tropoi**, and the Dorian octave (*e-e*) in two scales, **parupatai** and **ludia**. It is very possible (as was observed in commenting on them) that the two latter scales were in the key of *a*, and therefore Hypo-dorian in respect of mode. The Hypo-dorian mode is also exemplified by three at least of the instrumental passages given by the *Anonymus* (*supra*, p. 89).

2. The earliest trace of a difference of species appears to be found in the passage on the subject of the Mixo-lydian mode quoted above (p. 24) from Plutarch's *Dialogue on Music*. In that mode, according to Plutarch, it was discovered by a certain Lamprocles of Athens that the Disjunctive Tone was the highest interval, that is to say, that the octave in reality consisted of two conjunct tetrachords and a tone:

As the note which is the meeting-point of the two tetrachords is doubtless the key-note, we shall not be wrong in making it the Mesê, and thus finding the octave in question in the Perfect System and in the oldest part of it, viz. the tetrachords Mesôn and Synêmmenôn, with the Nêtê Diezeugmenôn. How then did this octave come to be recognised by Lamprocles as distinctively Mixo-lydian? We cannot tell with certainty, because we do not know what the Mixo-lydian scale was before his treatment of it. Probably, however, the answer is to be sought in the relation in respect of pitch between the Dorian and Mixo-lydian keys. These, as we have seen (p. 23), were the keys chiefly employed in tragedy, and the Mixo-lydian was a Fourth higher than the other. Now when a scale consisting of white notes is transposed to a key a Fourth higher, it becomes a scale with one b. In ancient language, the tetrachord Synêmmenôn (*a-bb-c-d*) takes the place of the tetrachord Diezeugmenôn. In some such way as this the octave of this form may have come to be associated in a special way with the use of the Mixo-lydian key.

- 80 -

However this may be, the change from the tetrachord Diezeugmenôn to the tetrachord Synêmmenôn, or the reverse, is a change of mode in the modern sense, for it is what the ancients classified as a change of System (**metabolê kata systêma**) [44]. Nor is it hard to determine the two 'modes' concerned, if we may trust to the authority of the Aristotelian *Problems* (*l. c.*) and regard the Mesê as always the key-note. For if *a* is kept as the key-note, the octave *a-a* with one ♭ is the so-called Dorian (*e-e* on the white notes). In this way we arrive at the somewhat confusing result that the ancient Dorian species (*e-e* but with *a* as key-note) yields the Hypo-dorian or modern Minor mode: while the Dorian mode of modern scientific theory [45] has its ancient prototype in the Mixo-lydian species, viz. the octave first brought to light by Lamprocles. The difficulty of course arises from the species of the Octave being classified according to their compass, without reference to the tonic character of the Mesê.

The Dorian mode is amply represented in the extant remains of Greek music. It is the mode of the two compositions of Dionysius, the Hymn to Calliope and the Hymn to Apollo (p. 88), perhaps also of Mr. Ramsay's musical inscription (p. 90). It would have been satisfactory if we could have found it in the much more important fragment of the *Orestes*. Such indications as that fragment presents seem to me to point to the Dorian mode (Mixo-lydian of Lamprocles).

3. The scales of the cithara furnish one example of the Phrygian species (*d-d*), and one of the Hypo-phrygian (*g-g*): but we have no means of determining which note of the scale is to be treated as the key-note.

In the Hymn to Nemesis, however, in spite of the incomplete form in which it has reached us, there is a sufficiently clear example of the Hypo-phrygian mode. It has been suggested as possible that the melody of Mr. Ramsay's inscription is also Hypo-phrygian, and if so the evidence for the mode would be carried back to the first century.

The Hypo-phrygian is the nearest approach made by any specimen of Greek music to the modern Major mode,—the Lydian or *c*-species not being found even among the scales of the cithara as given by Ptolemy. It is therefore of peculiar interest for musical history, and we look with eagerness for any indication which would allow us to connect it with the classical period of Greek art. One or two sayings of Aristotle have been thought to bear upon this issue.

The most interesting is a passage in the *Politics* (iv. 3, cp. p. 13), where Aristotle is speaking of the multiplicity of forms of government, and showing how a great number of varieties may nevertheless be brought under a few classes or types. He illustrates the point from the musical Modes, observing that all constitutions may be regarded as either oligarchical (government by a minority) or democratical (government by the majority), just as in the opinion of some musicians (**hôs phasi tines**) all modes are essentially either Dorian or Phrygian. What, then, is the basis of this grouping of certain modes together as Dorian, while the rest are Phrygian in character? According to Westphal it is a form of the opposition between the true Hellenic music, represented by Dorian, and the foreign music, the Phrygian and Lydian, with their varieties. Moreover, it is in his view virtually the same distinction as that which obtains in modern music between the Minor and the Major scales [46]. This account of the matter, however, is not supported by the context of the passage. Aristotle draws out the comparison between forms of government and musical modes in such a way as to make it plain that in the case of the modes the distinction was one of pitch (**tas suntonôteras ... tas d' aneimenas kai malakas**). The Dorian was the best, because the highest, of the lower keys,—the others being Hypo-dorian (in the earlier sense, immediately below Dorian), and Hypo-phrygian—while Phrygian was the first of the higher series which took in Lydian and Mixo-lydian. The division would be aided, or may even have been suggested, by the circumstance that it nearly coincided with the favourite contrast of Hellenic and 'barbarous' modes [47]. There is another passage, however, which can hardly be reconciled with a classification according to pitch alone. In the chapters dealing with the ethical character of music Aristotle dwells (as will be remembered) upon the exciting and orgiastic character of the Phrygian mode, and notices its especial fitness for the dithyramb. This fitness or affinity, he says, was so marked that a poet who tried to compose a dithyramb in another mode found himself passing unawares into the Phrygian (*Pol.* viii. 7). It is natural to understand this of the use of certain sequences of intervals, or of cadences, such as are characteristic of a 'mode' in the modern sense of the word, rather than of a change of key. If this is so we may venture the further hypothesis that the Phrygian music, in some at least of its forms, was distinguished not only by pitch, but also by the more or less conscious use of scales which differed in type from the scale of the Greek standard system.

It may be urged that this hypothesis is inconsistent with our interpretation of the passage of the *Problems* about the tonic character of the Mesê. If *a* is key-note, it was argued, the mode is that of the *a*-species (Hypo-dorian, our Minor), or at most—by admitting the tetrachord Synêmmenôn—it includes the *e*-species (Dorian of Helmholtz). The answer may be that the statement of the *Problems* is not of this absolute kind. It is not the statement of a technical writer, laying down definite rules, but is a general observation, or at best a canon of taste. We are not told how the predominance of the Mesê is shown in the form of the melody. Moreover this predominance is not said to be exercised in music generally, but in all *good* music (**panta gar ta chrêsta melê pollakis tê mesê chrêtai**). This may mean either that tonality in Greek music was of an imperfect kind, a question of style and taste rather than of fixed rule, or that they occasionally employed modes of a less approved stamp, unrecognised in the earlier musical theory.

---

# § 36. Conclusion.

The considerations set forth in the last chapter seem to show that if difference of mode or species cannot be entirely denied of the classical period of Greek music, it occupied a subordinate and almost unrecognised place.

The main elements of the art were, (1) difference of *genus*,—the sub-divisions of the tetrachord which Aristoxenus and Ptolemy alike recognise, though with important discrepancies in detail; (2) difference of pitch or *key*; and (3) *rhythm*. Passing over the last, as not belonging to the subject of *Harmonics*, we may now say that genus and key are the only grounds of distinction which are evidently of practical importance. No others were associated with the early history of the art, with particular composers or periods, with particular instruments, or with the ethos of music. This, however, is only true in the fullest sense of Greek music before the time of Ptolemy. The main object of Ptolemy's reform of the keys was to provide a new set of scales, each characterised by a particular succession of intervals, while the pitch was left to take care of itself. And it is clear, especially from the specimens which Ptolemy gives of the scales in use in his time, that he was only endeavouring to systematise what already existed, and bring theory into harmony with the developments of practice. We must suppose, therefore, that the musical feeling which sought variety in differences of key came to have less influence on the practical art, and that musicians began to discover, or to appreciate more than they had done, the use of different 'modes' or forms of the octave scale. Along with this change we have to note the comparative disuse of the Enharmonic and Chromatic divisions of the tetrachord. The Enharmonic, according to Ptolemy, had ceased to be employed. Of the three varieties of Chromatic given by Aristoxenus only one remains on Ptolemy's list, and that the one which in the scheme of Aristoxenus involved no interval less than a semitone. And although Ptolemy distinguished at least three varieties of Diatonic, it is worth notice that only one of these was admitted in the tuning of the lyre,—the others being confined to the more elaborate cithara. In Ptolemy's time, therefore, music was rapidly approaching the stage in which all its forms are based upon a single scale—the natural diatonic scale of modern Europe.

In the light of these facts it must occur to us that Westphal's theory of seven modes or species of the Octave is really open to an *a priori* objection as decisive in its nature as any of the testimony which has been brought against it. Is it possible, we may ask, that a system of modes analogous to the ecclesiastical Tones can have subsisted along with a system of scales such as the genera and 'colours' of early Greek music? The reply may be that Ptolemy himself combines the two systems. He supposes five divisions of the tetrachord, and seven modes based upon so many species of the Octave—

in all thirty-five different scales (or seventy, if we bring in the distinction of octaves **apo nêtês** and **apo mesês**). But when we come to the scales actually used on the chief Greek instrument, the cithara, the number falls at once to six. Evidently the others, or most of them, only existed on paper, as the mathematical results of certain assumptions which Ptolemy had made. And if this can be said of Ptolemy's theory, what would be the value of a similar scheme combining the modes with the Enharmonic and the different varieties of the Chromatic genus? The truth is, surely, that such a scheme tries to unite elements which belong to different times, which in fact are the fundamental ideas of different stages of art.

The most striking characteristic of Greek music, especially in its earlier periods, is the multiplicity and delicacy of the intervals into which the scale was divided. A sort of frame-work was formed by the division of the octave into tetrachords, completed by the so-called disjunctive tone; and so far all Greek music was alike. But within the tetrachord the reign of diversity was unchecked. Not only were there recognised divisions containing intervals of a fourth, a third, and even three-eighths of a tone, but we gather from several things said by Aristoxenus that the number of possible divisions was regarded as theoretically unlimited. Thus he tells us that there was a constant tendency to flatten the 'moveable' notes of the Chromatic genus, and thus diminish the small intervals, for the sake of 'sweetness' or in order to obtain a plaintive tone [48];— that the Lichanos of a tetrachord may in theory be any note between the Enharmonic Lichanos (*f* in the scale *e-e\*-f-a*) and the Diatonic (*g* in the scale *e-f-g-a*) [49];— and that the magnitude of the smaller intervals and division of the tetrachord generally belongs to the indefinite or indeterminate element in music [50]. Moreover, in spite of the disuse of several of the older scales, much of this holds good for the time of Ptolemy. The modern diatonic scale is fully recognised by him, but only as one of several different divisions. And the division which he treats as the ordinary or standard form of the octave is not the modern diatonic scale, but one of the so-called 'soft' or flattened varieties. It is clear that in the best periods of Greek music these refinements of melody, which modern musicians find scarcely conceivable, were far from being accidental or subordinate features. Rather, they were as much bound up with the fundamental nature of that music as complex harmony is with the music of modern Europe.

The mediaeval modes or Tones, on the other hand, are essentially based on the diatonic scale,—the scale that knows only of tones and semitones. To suppose that they held in the earliest Greek music the prominent place which we find assigned to the ancient Modes or **harmoniai** is to suppose that the art of music was developed in Greece in two different directions, under the influence of different and almost opposite ideas. Yet nothing is more remarkable in all departments of Greek art than the strictness with which it confines itself within the limits given once for all in the leading types, and the consequent harmony and consistency of all the forms which it takes in the course of its growth.

The dependence of artistic forms in their manifold developments upon a central governing idea or principle has never been more luminously stated than by the illustrious physicist Helmholtz, in the thirteenth chapter of his *Tonempfindungen*. I venture to think that in applying that truth to the facts of Greek music he was materially hindered by the accepted theory of the Greek modes. The scales which he analyses under that name were certainly the basis of all music in the Middle Ages, and are much more intelligible as such than in relation to the primitive Greek forms of the art [51].

# § 37. Epilogue—Speech and Song.

Several indications combine to make it probable that singing and speaking were not so widely separated from each other in Greek as in the modern languages with which we are most familiar.

(1) The teaching of the grammarians on the subject of accent points to this conclusion. Our habit of using Latin translations of the terms of Greek grammar has tended to obscure the fact that they belong in almost every case to the ordinary vocabulary of music. The word for 'accent' (**tonos**) is simply the musical term for 'pitch' or 'key.' The words 'acute' (**oxys**) and 'grave' (**barys**) mean nothing more than 'high' and 'low' in pitch. A syllable may have two accents, just as in music a syllable may be sung with more than one note. Similarly the 'quantity' of each syllable answers to the time of a musical note, and the rule that a long syllable is equal to two short ones is no doubt approximately correct. Consequently every Greek word (enclitics being reckoned as parts of a word) is a sort of musical phrase, and every sentence is a more or less definite melody—**logôdes ti melos**, as it is called by Aristoxenus (p. 18 Meib.). Moreover the accent in the modern sense, the *ictus* or stress of the voice, appears to be quite independent of the pitch or 'tonic' accent: for in Greek poetry the *ictus* (**arsis**) is determined by the metre, with which the tonic accent evidently has nothing to do. In singing, accordingly, the tonic accents disappear; for the melody takes their place, and gives each syllable a new pitch, on which (as we shall presently see) the spoken pitch has no influence. The rise and fall of the voice in ordinary speaking is perceptible enough in English, though it is more marked in other European languages. Helmholtz tells us—with tacit reference to the speech of North Germany—that an affirmative sentence generally ends with a drop in the tone of about a Fourth, while an interrogative is marked by a rise which is often as much as a Fifth [52]. In Italian the interrogative form is regularly given, not by a particle or a change in the order of the words, but by a rise of pitch. The Gregorian church music, according to a series of rules quoted by Helmholtz (*l. c.*), marked a comma by a rise of a Tone, a colon by a fall of a Semitone; a full stop by a Tone above, followed by a Fourth below, the 'reciting note'; and an interrogation by a phrase of the form *d b c d* (*c* being the reciting note).

These examples, however, do little towards enabling modern scholars to form a notion of the Greek system of accentuation. In these and similar cases it is the *sentence as a whole* which is modified by the tonic accent, whereas in Greek it is the individual *word*. It is true that the accent of a word may be affected by its place in the sentence: as is seen in the loss of the accent of oxytone words when not followed by a pause, in the anastrophe of prepositions, and in the treatment of the different classes of enclitics. But in all these instances it is the intonation of the word as such, not of the sentence, which is primarily concerned. What they really prove is that the musical accent is not so invariable as the stress accent in English or German, but may depend upon the collocation of the word, or upon the degree of emphasis which it has in a particular use.

(2) The same conclusion may be drawn from the terms in which the ancient writers on music endeavour to distinguish musical and ordinary utterance.

Aristoxenus begins his *Harmonics* by observing that there are two movements of the voice, not properly discriminated by any previous writer; namely, the *continuous*, which is the movement characteristic of speaking, and the *discrete* or that which proceeds by *intervals*, the movement of singing. In the latter the voice remains for a certain time on one note, and then passes by a definite interval to another. In the former it is continually gliding by imperceptible degrees from higher to lower or the reverse [53]. In this kind of movement the rise and fall of the voice is marked by the *accents* (**prosôdiai**), which accordingly form the melody, as it may be called, of spoken utterance [54]. Later writers state the distinction in much the same language. Nicomachus tells us that the two movements were first discriminated by the Pythagoreans. He dwells especially on the ease with which we pass from one to the other. If the notes and intervals of the speaking voice are allowed to be separate and distinct, the form of utterance becomes singing [55]. Similarly Aristoxenus says that we do not rest upon a note, unless we are led to do so by the influence of feeling (**an mê dia pathos pote eis toiautên kinêsin anankasthômen elthein**).

According to the rhetorician Dionysius of Halicarnassus the interval used in the melody of spoken utterance is approximately a Fifth, or three tones and a half (**dialektou men oun melos heni metreitai diastêmati tô legomenô dia pente, hôs engista; kai oute epiteinetai pera tôn triôn tonôn kai hêmitoniou epi to oxy oute anietai tou chôriou toutou pleion epi to bary** [56]). He gives an interesting example (quoted above on p. 91) from the *Orestes* of Euripides, to show that when words are set to music no account is taken of the accents, or spoken melody. Not merely are the intervals varied (instead of being nearly uniform), but the rise and fall of the notes does not answer to the rise and fall of the syllables in ordinary speech. This statement is rendered the more interesting from the circumstance that the inscription discovered by Mr. Ramsay (*supra*, p. 89), which is about a century later, does exhibit precisely this correspondence. Apparently, then, the melody of the inscription represents a new idea in music,—an attempt to bring it into a more direct connexion with the tones of the speaking voice. The fact of such an attempt being made seems to indicate that the divergence between the two kinds of utterance was becoming more marked than had formerly been the case. It may be compared with the invention of recitative in the beginning of the seventeenth century.

Aristides Quintilianus (p. 7 Meib.) recognises a third or intermediate movement of the voice, viz. that which is employed in the recitation of poetry. It is probable that Aristides is one of the latest writers on the subject, and we may conjecture that in his time the Greek language had in great measure lost the original tonic accents, and with them the quasi-melodious character which they gave to prose utterance.

In the view which these notices suggest the difference between speaking and singing is reduced to one of degree. It is analysed in language such as we might use to express the difference between a monotonous and a varied manner of speaking, or between the sounds of an Aeolian harp and those of a musical instrument.

(3) What has been said of melody in the two spheres of speech and song applies also *mutatis mutandis* to rhythm. In English the time or quantity of syllables is as little attended to as the pitch. But in Greek the distinction of long and short furnished a prose rhythm which was a serious element in their rhetoric. In the rhythm of music, according to Dionysius, the quantity of syllables could be neglected, just as the accent was neglected in the melody [57]. This, however, does not mean that the natural time of the syllables could be treated with the freedom which we see in a modern composition. The regularity of lyric metres is sufficient to prove that the increase or diminution of natural quantity referred to by Dionysius was kept within narrow limits, the nature of which is to be gathered from the remains of the ancient system of Rhythmic. From these sources we learn with something like certainty that the rhythm of ordinary speech, as determined by the succession of long or short syllables, was the basis not only of metres intended for recitation, such as the hexameter and the iambic trimeter, but also of lyrical rhythm of every kind.

(4) As to the use of the stress accent in Greek prose we are without direct information. In verse it appears as the metrical *ictus* or *arsis* of each foot, which answers to what English musicians call the 'strong beat' or accented part of the bar [58]. In the Homeric hexameter the ictus is confined to long syllables, and appears to have some power of lengthening a short or doubtful syllable. In the Attic poetry which was written in direct imitation of colloquial speech, viz. the tragic and comic trimeter, there is no necessary connexion

between the ictus and syllabic length: but on the other hand a naturally long syllable which is without the ictus may be rhythmically short. In lyrical versification the ictus does not seem to have any connexion with quantity: and on the whole we may gather that it was not until the Byzantine period of Greek that it came to be recognised as a distinct factor in pronunciation. The chief elements of utterance—pitch, time and stress—were independent in ancient Greek speech, just as they are in music. And the fact that they were independent goes a long way to prove our main contention, viz. that ancient Greek speech had a peculiar quasi-musical character, consequently that the difficulty which modern scholars feel in understanding the ancient statements on such matters as accent and quantity is simply the difficulty of conceiving a form of utterance of which no examples can now be observed.

The conception which we have thus been led to form of ancient Greek as it was spoken is not without bearing on the main subject of these pages. For if the language even in its colloquial form had qualities of rhythm and intonation which gave it this peculiar half musical character, so that singing and speaking were more closely akin than they ever are in our experience, we may expect to find that music was influenced in some measure by this state of things. What is there, then, in the special characteristics of Greek music which can be connected with the exceptional relation in which it stood to language?

Greek music was primarily and chiefly vocal. Instrumental music was looked upon as essentially subordinate,—an accompaniment or at best an imitation of singing. For in the view of the Greeks the words (**lexis**) were an integral part of the whole composition. They contained the ideas, while the music with its variations of time (**rhythmos**) and pitch (**harmonia**) furnished a natural vehicle for the appropriate feelings. Purely instrumental music could not do this, because it could not convey the ideas or impressions fitted to be the object of feeling. Hence we find Plato complaining on this ground of the separation of poetry and music which was beginning to be allowed in his time. The poets, he says, rend asunder the elements of music; they separate rhythm and dance movements from melody, putting unmusical language into metre, and again make melody and rhythm without words, employing the lyre and the flute without the voice: so that it is most difficult, when rhythm and melody is produced without language, to know what it means, or what subject worthy of the name it represents (**kai hotô eoike tôn axiologôn mimêmatôn**). It is utterly false taste, in Plato's opinion, to use the flute or the lyre otherwise than as an accompaniment to dance and song [59]. Similarly in the Aristotelian *Problems* (xix. 10) it is asked why, although the human voice is the most pleasing, singing without words, as in humming or whistling, is not more agreeable than the flute or the lyre. Shall we say, the writer answers, 'that the human voice too is comparatively without charm if it does not *represent* something? (**ê oud' ekei, ean mê mimêtai, homoiôs hêdy?**) That is to say, music is expressive of *feeling*, which may range from acute passion to calm and lofty sentiment, but feeling must have an object, and this can only be adequately given by language. Thus language is, in the first instance at least, the matter to which musical treatment gives artistic form. In modern times the tendency is to regard instrumental music as the highest form of the art, because in instrumental music the artist creates his work, not by taking ideas and feelings as he finds them already expressed in language, but directly, by forming an independent vehicle of feeling,—a new language, as it were, of passion and sentiment,—out of the absolute relations of movement and sound.

The intimate connexion in Greek music between words and melody may be shown in various particulars. The modern practice of basing a musical composition—a long and elaborate chorus, for example—upon a few words, which are repeated again and again as the music is developed, would have been impossible in Greece.

It becomes natural when the words are not an integral part of the work, but only serve to announce the idea on which it is based, and which the music brings out under successive aspects. The same may be said of the use of a melody with many different sets of words. Greek writers regard even the repetition of the melody in a strophe and antistrophe as a concession to the comparative weakness of a chorus. With the Greeks, moreover, the union in one artist of the functions of poet and musician must have tended to a more exquisite adaptation of language and music than can be expected when the work of art is the product of divided labour. In Greece the principle of the interdependence of language, metre, and musical sound was carried very far. The different recognised styles had each certain metrical forms and certain musical scales or keys appropriated to them, in some cases also a certain dialect and vocabulary. These various elements were usually summed up in an ethnical type, one of those which played so large a part in their political history. Such a term as Dorian was not applied to a particular scale at random, but because that scale was distinctive of Dorian music: and Dorian music, again, was one aspect of Dorian temper and institutions, Dorian literature and thought.

Whether the Greeks were acquainted with harmony—in the modern sense of the word—is a question that has been much discussed, and may now be regarded as settled [60]. It is clear that the Greeks were acquainted with the phenomena on which harmony depends, viz. the effect produced by sounding certain notes together. It appears also that they made some use of harmony,—and of dissonant as well as consonant intervals,—in instrumental accompaniment (**krousis**).

On the other hand it was unknown in their vocal music, except in the form of bass and treble voices singing the same melody. In the instrumental accompaniment it was only an occasional ornament, not a necessary or regular part of the music. Plato speaks of it in the *Laws* as something which those who learn music as a branch of liberal education should not attempt [61]. The silence of the technical writers, both as to the use of harmony and as to the tonality of the Greek scale, points in the same direction. Evidently there was no *system* of harmony,—no notion of the effect of *successive* harmonies, or of two distinct *parts* or progressions of notes harmonising with each other.

The want of harmony is to be connected not only with the defective tonality which was probably characteristic of Greek music,—we have seen (p. 42) that there is some evidence of tonality,—but still more with the non-harmonic quality of many of the intervals of which their scales were composed. We have repeatedly dwelt upon the variety and strangeness (to our apprehension) of these intervals. Modern writers are usually disposed to underrate their importance, or even to explain them away. The Enharmonic, they point out, was produced by the interpolation of a note which may have been only a passing note or *appoggiatura*. The Chromatic also, it is said, was regarded as too difficult for ordinary performers, and most of its varieties went out of use at a comparatively early period. Yet the accounts which we find in writers so remote in time and so opposed in their theoretical views as Aristoxenus and Ptolemy, bear the strongest testimony to the reality and persistence of these non-diatonic scales.

And we have the decisive fact that of the six scales of the cithara given by Ptolemy (see p. 85) not one is diatonic in the modern sense of the word. It may be alleged on the other side that the ideal scale in the *Timaeus* of Plato is purely diatonic, and exhibits the strictest Pythagorean division. But that scale is primarily a framework of mathematical ratios, and could not take notice of intervals which had not yet been identified with ratios. It is not certain when the discovery of Pythagoras was extended to the non-diatonic scales. Even in the *Sectio Canonis* of Euclid there is no trace of knowledge that any intervals except those of the Pythagorean diatonic scale had a numerical or (as we should say) physical basis [62]. In Plato's time, as we can see from a well-known passage of the *Republic* (quoted on p. 53), the Enharmonic and

Chromatic scales were the object of much zealous study and experiment on the part of musicians of different schools,—some seeking to measure and compare the intervals directly by the ear, others to find numbers in the consonances which they heard, and both, from the Platonic point of view, 'setting ears above intelligence,' and therefore labouring in vain [63].

The multiplicity of intervals, then, which surprises us in the doctrine of the *genera* and 'colours' was not an accident or excrescence. And although some of the finer varieties, such as the Enharmonic, belong only to the early or classical period, there is enough to show that it continued to be characteristic of the Greek musical system, at least until the revival of Hellenism in the age of the Antonines. The grounds of this peculiarity may be sought partly in the Greek temperament. We can hardly deny the Greeks the credit of a fineness of sensibility upon which civilisation, to say the least, has made no advance. We may note further how entirely it is in accordance with the analogies of Greek art to find a series of artistic types created by subtle variations within certain well-defined limits. For the present purpose, however, it will be enough to consider how the phenomenon is connected with other known characteristics of Greek music,—its limited compass and probably imperfect tonality, the thin and passionless quality of its chief instrument, on the other hand the keen sense of differences of pitch, the finely constructed rhythm, and finally the natural adaptation, on which we have already dwelt, between the musical form and the language.

The last is perhaps the feature of greatest significance, especially in a comparison of the ancient and modern types of the art. The beauty and even the persuasive effect of a voice depend, as we are more or less aware, in the first place upon the pitch or key in which it is set, and in the second place upon subtle variations of pitch, which give emphasis, or light and shade. Answering to the first of these elements ancient music, if the main contention of this essay is right, has its system of Modes or keys. Answering to the second it has a series of scales in which the delicacy and variety of the intervals still fill us with wonder. In both these points modern music shows diminished resources. We have in the Keys the same or even a greater command of degrees of pitch: but we seem to have lost the close relation which once obtained between a note as the result of physical facts and the same note as an index of temper or emotion. A change of key affects us, generally speaking, like a change of colour or of movement—not as the heightening or soothing of a state of feeling. In respect of the second element of vocal expression, the rise and fall of the pitch, Greek music possessed in the multiplicity of its scales a range of expression to which there is no modern parallel. The nearest analogue may be found in the use of modulation from a Major to a Minor key, or the reverse. But the changes of genus and 'colour' at the disposal of an ancient musician must have been acoustically more striking, and must have come nearer to reproducing, in an idealised form, the tones and inflexions of the speaking voice. The tendency of music that is based upon harmony is to treat the voice as one of a number of instruments, and accordingly to curtail the use of it as the great source of dramatic and emotional effect. The consequence is twofold. On the one hand we lose sight of the direct influence exerted by sound of certain degrees of pitch on the human sensibility, and thus ultimately on character. On the other hand the music becomes an independent creation. It may still be a vehicle of the deepest feeling: but it no longer seeks the aid of language, or reaches its aim through the channels by which language influences the mind of man.

# APPENDIX

## TABLE I.

*Scales of the seven oldest Keys, with the species of the same name.*

Mixo-lydian.    *b*-species.

Lydian.    *c*-species.

Phrygian.    *d*-species.

Dorian.    *e*-species.

Hypo-lydian.    *f*-species.

Hypo-phrygian.    *g*-species.

Hypo-dorian.    *a*-species.

[Listen: Mixo-lydian]    [Listen: Lydian]    [Listen: Phrygian]

[Listen: Dorian]    [Listen: Hypo-lydian]    [Listen: Hypo-phrygian]

[Listen: Hypo-dorian]

## TABLE II.

*The fifteen Keys.*

Mesê.
Hyper-lydian.
Hyper-aeolian.
Hyper-phrygian.
Hyper-ionian.
Mixo-lydian.
Lydian.
Aeolian.
Phrygian.
Ionian.

**Dorian.**

**Hypo-lydian.**

**Hypo-aeolian.**

**Hypo-phrygian.**

**Hypo-ionian.**

**Hypo-dorian.**

[Listen: Hyper-lydian]   [Listen: Hyper-aeolian]   [Listen: Hyper-phrygian]

[Listen: Hyper-ionian]   [Listen: Mixo-lydian]   [Listen: Lydian]

[Listen: Aeolian]   [Listen: Phrygian]   [Listen: Ionian]

[Listen: Dorian]   [Listen: Hypo-lydian]   [Listen: Hypo-aeolian]

[Listen: Hypo-phrygian]   [Listen: Hypo-ionian]   [Listen: Hypo-dorian]

*Transcriber's* *Note:*
Corrected final note in "Lydian" midi file from E as written to F as is more
logical.

The moveable notes (**phthongoi kinoumenoi**) are distinguished by being
printed as crotchets.

The two highest of these keys—the Hyper-lydian and the Hyper-aeolian—appear to have been added in the time of the Empire. The remaining thirteen are attributed to Aristoxenus in the pseudo-Euclidean *Introductio* (p. 19, l. 30), and by Aristides Quintilianus (p. 22, l. 30): but there is no mention of them in the extant *Harmonics*. It may be gathered, however, from the criticism of Heraclides Ponticus (see the passage discussed on pp. 9-12) that the list of keys was being considerably enlarged in his time, and Aristoxenus, though not named, is doubtless aimed at there. Music of the 'Orestes' of Euripides (ll. 338-344).

κατολοφ **Π̄ Ρ C · Ρ· Φ Π** ΥΡΟΜΑΙΖΜΑΤΕΡΟΣ αἷμα σᾶς

ὅ σ' ἀναβ **Z(?) ·Ι' ·Z E E(?)** ΑΚΧΕΥΕΙΖΟΜΕΓΑΣ ὄλβος οὐ

μόνιμο **Π̄ Ρ C · Ι· Z** ΣΕΜΒΡΟΤΟΙΣΖ ΑΝΑ δὲ λαῖφος

ὥς τι **C Ρ Π̄ C Ρ Ζ Φ· C,** ΣΑΚΑΤΟΥΘΟΑΣΤΙΝΑξας δαί-

μων **Φ· Π Ρ Π̄** ΚΑΤΕΚΛΥΣΕΝℸ Ↄ δεινῶν

πόνω **Ζ̇ Ι·Ⴟ. Z Φ** ΝℸↃΩΩΣΠΟΝΤου

**I C: C: PvZ(?) Φ(?)**
ὀλεθρΙοιΣΙΝ ἐν κύμασιν

Restoration proposed by Dr. Crusius.

κατ - ο - λο - φύ - ρο - μαι    μα - τέ - ρος    αἷ - μα σᾶς

ὅ σ' ἀνα - βακ - χεύ - ει.    ὁ μέ - γας    ὄλ - βος οὐ

[Listen]

kat-o-lo-phu-ro-mai ma-te-ros ai-ma sas
o s ana-bak-cheu-ei. o me-gas ol-bos ou
mon-i-mos en Bro-tois a-na de lai-phos hôs
tis a-ka-tou tho-as ti-na-xas dai-môn
kat-ek-ly-sen dei-nôn po-nôn hôs pon-tou
lab-rois o-leth-ri-oi-sin en ky-ma-sin

The metre is dochmiac, each dochmius consisting of an iambus followed by

a cretic, ⏑ — — ⏑ — . The points which seem to mark the ictus, or rhythmical accent, are found on the first syllable of each of these two feet. If we assume that the first syllable of the iambus has the chief accent, the dochmius will be correctly expressed as a musical bar of the form—

If the first syllable of the cretic is accented, the dochmius is divided between two bars, and becomes—

The accompaniment or **krousis**, consisting of notes interposed between the phrases of the melody, is found by Dr. Wessely and Dr. Crusius in the following characters:

1. The character  appears at the end of every dochmius shown by the papyrus. After the first, third and fifth it is written in the same line with the text. After the seventh it is written above that line, between two vocal notes. Dr. Crusius takes it to be the instrumental **Z**, explaining the difference of shape as due to the necessity or convenience of distinguishing it from the

vocal **Z**. If that were so the form  would surely have been permanent, and would have been given in the schemes of Alypius and Aristides Quintilianus. I venture to suggest that it is a mark intended to show the end of the dochmius or bar.

2. The group  occurs twice, before and after the words **deinôn ponôn**. There is a difficulty about the sign , which Dr. Crusius takes to be a *Vortragszeichen*. The other two characters may be instrumental notes.

The double ω of ως (written ΩΩΣ) is interesting because it shows that when more than one note went with a syllable, the vowel or diphthong was repeated. This agrees with the well-known **hei-ei-ei-ei-ei-eilissete** of Aristophanes (*Ran.* 1314), and is amply confirmed by the newly discovered hymn to Apollo (p. 134).

*Musical part of the Seikelos inscription.*

ΟΣΟΝΖΗΣΦΑΙΝΟΥ

ΜΗΔΕΝΟΛΩΣΣΥ

ΛΥΠΟΥΠΡΟΣΟΛΙ

ΓΟΝΕΣΤΙΤΟΖΗΝ

ΤΟΤΕΛΟΣΟΧΡΟ

ΝΟΣΑΠΑΙΤΕΙ

OSONZÊSPHAINOU MÊDENOLÔSSY LYPOUPOSOLI
GONESTITOZÊN TOTELOSOCHRO NOSAPAITEI

The inscription of which these lines form part was discovered by Mr. W. M. Ramsay, and was first published by him in the *Bulletin de correspondance hellénique* for 1883, p. 277. It professes to be the work of a certain **Seikelos**.

The discovery that the smaller letters between the lines are musical notes was made by Dr. Wessely.

The Seikelos inscription, as Dr. O. Crusius has shown (*Philologus* for 1893, LII. p. 161), is especially valuable for the light which it throws upon ancient rhythm. The quantity of the syllables and the place of the *ictus* is marked in every case, and we are able therefore to divide the melody into bars, which may be represented as follows:

ὅσον | ζῆς φαί- | νου· μηδὲν | ὅλως σὺ λυ- | ποῦ· πρὸς ὀλί- |

γον ἐστὶ τὸ | ζῆν· τὸ τέλος | ὁ χρόνος ἀπαι- | τεῖ.

**hoson | zês phai-| nou; mêden | holôs sy ly-| pou; pros oli-| gon esti to | zên; to telos | ho chronos apai-| tei.**

*The hymns recently discovered at Delphi.*

Since these sheets were in type the materials for the study of ancient Greek music have received a notable accession. The French archaeologists who are now excavating on the site of Delphi have found several important fragments of lyrical poetry, some of them with the music noted over the words, as in the examples already known. The two largest of these fragments have been shown to belong to a single inscription, containing a hymn to Apollo, which dates in all probability from the early part of the third century B. C. Of the other fragments the most considerable is plausibly referred to the first century B. C. These inscriptions have been published in the *Bulletin de correspondance hellénique* (viii-xii. pp. 569-610), with two valuable commentaries by M. Henri Weil and M. Théodore Reinach. The former scholar deals with the text, the latter chiefly with the music.

The music of the hymn to Apollo is written in the vocal notation. The metre is the cretic or paeonic , and the key, as M. Reinach has shown, is the Phrygian—the scale of C minor, with the conjunct tetrachord *c—db—d—f.*

In the following transcription I have followed M. Reinach except in a few minor points. When two notes are sung to the same syllable the vowel or diphthong is repeated, as in the fragment of the Orestes (p. 132): but I have thought it best to adhere to the modern method.

A

[Τὸν κιθαρί]σει κλυ-τὸν παῖ-δα με-γά-λου [Διὸς ἀ-

εἴδετε πα]ρ' ἀ-κρο-νι-φῆ τόν-δε πά-γον, ἄμ[βροθ' ὃς]

πᾶ-σι θνα-τοῖς προ-φαί-νεις [λόγια, τρ]ί-πο-δα μαν-

τεῖ-ον ὡς εἷ[λες, ἐχθρὸς ὃν ἐ-φρ]ού-ρει δρά-κων·

ὅ-τε τε[οῖσι βέλεσιν ἔ-τρ]η-σας αἰ-ό-λον ἕ-λικ-τὰν [

] συ-ρίγ-μαθ' ἱ-είς ἀ-θώ-πε[υτ' ἔβα·

νῦν] δὲ Γα-λα-τᾶν ἄ-ρης ..ν ἐπέ-ρασ' ἀ-σεπ-τ[ος

σαλ-λι-ω (?) γέν-ναν ..ν θάλος φί-λον

δά-μοι-ο λο.. ..ρων ἔ-φορ..

τε-ον κ.. ε-ναι κ..

(about 12 bars wanting.)

B    I   Μ Υ Μ      ⊙ Ι Μ

Ἑλικ]ῶνα βα - θύ - δεν - δρον αἳ    λά[χετε Διὸς ἐρι]βρό - μου

I Μ Υ Μ     ⊙    ⊙   Ι Μ Ι

θύ - γα-τρες εὐ - ώ - λε[νοι] μό - λε[τε] συν-ό - μαι-μον ἵ - να

Μ Υ Μ Υ Μ F Φ Υ F

Φοῖ - βον ᾠ - διῖ - σι μέλ - ψη - τε χρυ - σε - ο - κό - μαν·

⊙    Ʊ ⅄ Ʊ ⊙   Ʊ    ⊙    Μ ⊙

ὃς ἀ - νὰ δι - κο - ρύ - νι - α Παρ-νασ - σί-δος τᾶσ - δε πέτ -

Ι    Μ Υ    Μ Υ Μ Ι ⊙ Ι ⊙ Γ Ʊ ⅄ Γ

- ρας ἕ - δρα-να [με]τὰ κλυ - ταῖς Δελ - φί-σιν Κασ-τα-λί-δος

Ʊ ⅄ Ʊ    ⊙ Γ     Λ      Μ

εὐ - ύ-δρου νά - ματ' ἐ - πι - νί - σε-ται, Δελ-φὸν ἀ - νὰ

Υ    Μ Ι ⊙ Ι Μ    Φ       Γ

[πρ]ῶ - να μαν - τεῖ - ον ἐ - φέ - πων πά - γον. [ἴθι] κλυτὰ

[Listen]

Ton kithari]sei kly-ton pai-da me-ga-lou [Dios a-] eidete pa]r' a-kro-ni-phê ton-de pa-gon, am[broth' hos] pa-si thna-tois pro-phai-neis [logia, tr]i-po-da man- tei-on hôs hei[les, echthros hon e-phr]ou-rei dra-kôn; ho-te te[oisi belesin e-tr]ê-sas ai-o-lon he-lik-tan sy-rig-math' hi-eis a-thô-pe[ut' eba; nyn] de Ga-la-tan a-rês..n epe-ras' a-sep-t[os] sal-li-ô](?) gen-nan..n thalos phi-lon da-moi-o lo....rôn e-phor.. te-on k.. e-nai k.. ôna ba-thy-den-dron hai la[chete Dios eri]bro-mou thy-ga-tres eu-ô-le[noi] mo-le[te] syn-o-mai-mon hi-na

- 106 -

Phoi-bon ô-dai-si mel-psê-te chry-se-o-ko-man; hos a-na di-ko-ry-ni-
a Par-nas-si-dos tas-de pet- -ras he-dra-na [me]ta kly-tais Del-phi-sin
Kas-ta-li-dos eu-u-drou na-mat' e-pi-ni-se-tai, Del-phon a-na [pr]ô-
na man-tei-on e-phe-pôn pa-gon. [ithi] klyta me-ga-lo-po-lis Aththis, eu-chai-si phe-ro-ploi-o nai- -ou-sa Tri-tô-ni-dos da[ped]on a-
thrauston, ha-gi- -ois de bô-moi-sin Ha-phais-tos ai-thei ne-ôn mê-ra
tau-rôn; ho-mou de nin A-raps at-mos es Y- -lym-pon a-na-kid-na-
tai; li-gy de lô-tos bre-môn ai-o-lois [me]le-sin ô-dan kre-kei; chry-
sea d' ha-dy-throu[s ki]-tha-ris hym-noi-sin a-na-mel-pe-tai; ho de
[the]-ô-rôn pro-pas es-mos Ath-thi-da lach[ôn]

The notes employed in this piece of music cover about an octave and a half,
viz. from Parypatê Hypatôn to the Chromatic Lichanos Hyperbolaiôn. In
two of the tetrachords, viz. Synemmenôn and Hyperbolaiôn, the intervals
employed are Chromatic (or possibly Enharmonic): in the tetrachord
Diezeugmenôn they are Diatonic, while in the tetrachord Mesôn the
Lichanos, which would distinguish the genus, is wanting. On the other hand
there are two notes which do not belong to the Phrygian key as hitherto
known, viz. **O**, a semitone below Mesê, and **B**, a semitone below Nêtê
Diezeugmenôn. If we assume that we have before us Chromatic of the
standard kind (**chrôma toniaion**), the complete scale is—

[Listen]

[Listen]

If the intervals are Enharmonic, or Chromatic of a different variety, the
moveable notes (in this case **Λ Κ** and , **Λ ✳** ) will be somewhat
flatter.

M. Reinach is particularly happy in tracing the successive changes of genus
and key in the course of the poem. The opening passage, as he shows, is

Diatonic. With the mention of the Gaulish invasion (**Galatan arês**) we come upon the group ℧ 𝗔 ✳ (*g—ab—a*) of the Chromatic tetrachord Hyperbolaiôn. At the beginning of the second fragment the intervals are again Diatonic, up to the point where the poet turns to address the Attic procession (**ithi, klyta megalopolis Aththis, k.t.l.**). From this point the melody lies chiefly in the Chromatic tetrachord Synemmenôn **M 𝗔 K Γ** (*c—db—d—f*)—a modulation into the key of the sub-dominant as well as a change of genus. At the end of the fragment the poet returns to the Diatonic and the original key. With regard to the *mode*—the question which mainly concerns us at present—M. Reinach's exposition is clear and convincing. He appeals to three criteria,—(1) the impression which the music makes on a modern ear; (2) the endings of the several phrases and divisions; and (3) the note which recurs most frequently. All these criteria point to a Minor mode. The general impression made by the Diatonic parts of the melody is that of the key of *C* minor: the rhythmical periods end on one or other of the notes *c-eb-g*, which form the chord of that key: and the note *c* distinctly predominates. This conclusion, it need hardly be said, is in entire agreement with the main thesis of the preceding pages.

The symbols **O** and **B**, which do not belong to the Phrygian scale, are explained by M. Reinach in a way that is in a high degree plausible and suggestive. In other keys, he observes, the symbol **O** stands for the note *b* (natural). Thus it holds the place of 'leading-note' (*note sensible*) to the keynote, *c*. It has hitherto been supposed that the standard scale of Greek music, the octave *a-a*, differed from the modern Minor in the want of a leading note. Here, however, we find evidence that such a note was known in practice, if not as a matter of theory, to Greek musicians. If this is so, it strongly confirms the view that *c* was in fact the key-note of the Phrygian scale. The symbol **B**, which occurs only once, answers to our *gb*, and may be similarly explained as a leading note to *g*, the dominant of the key. We infer, with M. Reinach, that the scale employed in the hymn is not only like, but identical with, the scale of our Minor.

The fragment marked **C** by M. Weil resembles the hymn to Apollo in subject, and also in metre, but cannot belong to the same work. The melody is written in the Lydian key, with the notation which we have hitherto known as the instrumental, but which is now shown to have been used, occasionally at least, for vocal music. The fragment is as follows:

[Listen]

**t' e-pi tê-les-ko-pon tan[de] di-ko-ry-phon klei-tyn hym[in] Pi-erides
ai ni-pho-bo-lous mel-pe-te de Py-thi-on Phoi-bon on e-tik-te L[a-tô]**

M. Reinach connects this fragment with a shorter one, also in the Lydian key,
but not in paeonic metre, viz.—

[Listen]

**.. thon es-che ma ... thê-ra kat-ek-ta.... syrigm' a-per..**

M. Reinach thinks that the mode may be the so-called Hypo-lydian (the
octave *f—f*). The materials are surely too scanty for any conclusion as to this.

The fragment D, the only remaining piece which M. Reinach has found it
worth while to transcribe, is also written in the instrumental notation of the
Lydian key. The metre is the glyconic. The fragment is as follows:—

[Listen]

ton man-to-sy[na klyton] ô-leth' hy-gra ch ... despoti Krê-siôn .. ai
nae-tas Delphôn ...in ap-tais-tous Bak-chou [thiasous] ... te
prospolois tan te do[u]ri[klytôn ar-chan au-xet' a-gê-ra-tô thal ...

This piece also is referred by M. Reinach to the Hypo-lydian mode. It may
surely be objected that of three places in which we may fairly suppose that
we have the end of a metrical division, viz. those which end with the words
**Delphôn, prospolois** and **agêratô**, two present us with cadences on the
Mesê (*d*), and one on the Hypatê (*a*). This seems to point strongly to the
Minor Mode.

On the whole it would seem that the only *mode* (in the modern sense of the
word) of which the new discoveries tell us anything is a mode practically

identical with the modern Minor. I venture to think this a confirmation, as signal as it was unexpected, of the main contention of this treatise.

It does not seem to have been observed by M. Weil or M. Reinach that in all these pieces of music there is the same remarkable correspondence between the melody and the accentuation that has been pointed out in the case of the Seikelos inscription (pp. 90, 91). It cannot indeed be said that every acute accent coincides with a rise of pitch: but the note of an accented syllable is almost always followed by a note of lower pitch. Exceptions are, **aiolon, hina** (which may have practically lost its accent, cp. the Modern Greek **na**), and **molete** (if rightly restored). The fall of pitch in the two notes of a circumflexed syllable is exemplified in **manteion, heilen, Galatan, Phoibon, ôdaisi, klytais, bômoisin, homou:** the opposite case occurs only once, in **thnatois.** The observation holds not only of the chief hymn, but of all the fragments.

---

*Note on the Seikilos Inscription* (pp. 89-91, 133).

---

Since the publication of this work, the Seikilos inscription has been examined afresh by Mr. J. A. R. Munro (of Lincoln College, Oxford). The result of his examination is to show that the last note of the melody has been misread. From a squeeze which he has kindly placed at my disposal it appears that the word **apaitei** is written—

$$\mathsf{c \qquad \bar{c} \quad c\underset{\smile}{x}\dot{\daleth}}$$

$$\mathsf{A\Pi AITEI}$$

The line drawn under the three notes $\mathsf{c x \daleth}$ has caused the last to be read as $\daleth$ , which has no meaning here. In fact it is a reversed Gamma (**g apestrammenon**), and answers to our *e* natural.

Hence the last line of the transcription on pp. 89-90 should be as follows:

to te-los ho chro-nos a-pai—tei

[Listen]

The importance of this correction is obvious. The scale employed is now seen to be the octave—

$$e \quad f\sharp \quad g \quad a \quad b \quad c\sharp \quad d \quad e$$

If, as I ventured to suggest on p. 90, the mode is the Hypo-phrygian (the scale of our Major mode, but with a flat Seventh), the key-note will be *a*. The close on the Dominant *e* will then have to be noted as a fact supporting the belief that in Greek music the close on the Dominant or Hypatê was the usual one (see p. 45).

The line drawn under the three symbols ⸢ΧꞀ᛫ is found in several other cases where the melody gives more than one note for a syllable. So ΙΚ (l. 2), and ΟΦ (l. 3), ΚΙ and ΟΦ (l. 4). It does not appear however under ΚΙΖ (l. 1).

D. B. M.

# FOOTNOTES

[1] Plato, *Rep.* p. 400 *b* **alla tauta men, ên d' egô, kai meta Damônos bouleusometha, tines te aneleutherias kai hybreôs ê manias kai allês kakias prepousai baseis, kai tinas tois enantiois leipteon rhythmous.**

[2] It is foreign to our purpose to discuss the critical problems presented by the text of Aristoxenus. Of the three extant books the first is obviously a distinct treatise, and should probably be entitled **peri archôn.** The other two books will then bear the old title **harmonika stoicheia.** They deal with the same subjects, for the most part, as the first book, and in the same order,— a species of repetition of which there are well-known instances in the Aristotelian writings. The conclusion is abrupt, and some important topics are omitted. It seems an exaggeration, however, to describe the *Harmonics* of Aristoxenus as a mere collection of excerpts, which is the view taken by Marquard (*Die harmonischen Fragmente des Aristoxenus*, pp. 359-393). See Westphal's *Harmonik und Melopöie der Griechen* (p. 41, ed. 1863), and the reply to Marquard in his *Aristoxenus von Tarent* (pp. 165-170). is not given in the *Harmonics* which we have: but we find there what is in some respects more valuable, namely, a vivid account of the state of things in respect of tonality which he observed in the music of his time.

[3] *Harm.* p. 37, 19 Meib. **houtô gar hoi men tôn harmonikôn legousi barytaton men ton Hypodôrion tôn tonôn, hêmitoniô de oxyteron toutou ton Mixolydion, toutou de hêmitoniô ton Dôrion, tou de Dôriou tonô ton Phrygion: hôsautôs de kai tou Phrygiou ton Lydion heterô tonô.** Westphal (*Harmonik und Melopöie* p. 165) would transfer the words **hêmitoniô ... Mixolydion** to the end of the sentence, and insert **oxyteron** before **ton Dôrion.** The necessity for this insertion shows that Westphal's transposition is not in itself an easy one. The only reason for it is the difficulty of supposing that there could have been so great a difference in the pitch of the Mixo-lydian scale. As to this, however, see p. 23 (note).

The words **Hypophrygion aulon** have also been condemned by Westphal (*Aristoxenus*, p. 453). He points out the curious contradiction between **pros tên tôn aulôn trypêsin blepontes** and the complaint **ti d' esti pros ho blepontes ... ouden eirêkasin.** But if **pros tên ... blepontes** was a marginal gloss, as Westphal suggests, it was doubtless a gloss on **aulon**, and if so, **aulon** is presumably sound. Since the **aulos** was especially a Phrygian instrument, and regularly associated with the Phrygian mode (as we know from Aristotle, see p. 13), nothing is more probable than that there was a variety of flute called Hypo-phrygian, because tuned so as to yield the Hypo-phrygian key, either by itself or as a modulation from the Phrygian.

In this scheme the important feature—that which marks it as an advance on the others referred to by Aristoxenus—is the conformity which it exhibits with the diatonic scale. The result of this conformity is that the keys stand in a certain relation to each other. Taking any two, we find that certain notes are common to them. So long as the intervals of pitch were quite arbitrary, or were practically irrational quantities, such as three-quarters of a tone, no such relation could exist. It now became possible to pass from one key to another, *i. e.* to employ *modulation* (**metabolê**) as a source of musical effect. This new system had evidently made some progress when Aristoxenus wrote, though it was not perfected, and had not passed into general use.

[4] An objection to this identification has been based on the words of Pollux, *Onom.* iv. 78 **kai harmonia men aulêtikê Dôristi, Phrygisti, Lydios kai Iônikê, kai syntonos Lydisti ên Anthippos exeure.** The source of this statement, or at least of the latter part of it, is evidently the same as that of the notice in Plutarch. The agreement with Plato's list makes it probable that this source was some comment on the passage in the *Republic*. If so, it can hardly be doubted that Pollux gives the original terms, the Platonic **Lydisti** and **Syntonolydisti**, and consequently that the later Lydian is not to be found in his **Lydios** (which is a 'relaxed' mode), but in his **syntonos Lydisti**. There is no difficulty in supposing that the mode was called **syntonos** merely in contrast to the other.

[5] It seems not impossible that this difficulty with regard to the 'slack Lydian' and Hypo-lydian may be connected with the contradiction in the statement of Aristoxenus about the schemes of keys in his time (p. 18). According to that account, if the text is sound, some musicians placed the Mixo-lydian a semitone below the Dorian—the Hypo-dorian being again a semitone lower. In this scheme, then, the Mixo-lydian held the place of the later Hypo-lydian. The conjecture may perhaps be hazarded, that this lower Mixo-lydian somehow represents Plato's 'slack Lydian,' and eventually passed into the Hypo-lydian.

[6] Aristides Quintilianus uses **tropos** as the regular word for 'key:' e.g. in p. 136 **en tê tôn tropôn, hous kai tonous ekalesamen, ekthesei.** So Alypius (p. 2 Meib.) **dielein eis tous legomenous tropous te kai tonous, ontas pentekaideka ton arithmon.** Also Bacchius in his catechism (p. 12 Meib.) **hoi tous treis tropous adontes tinas adousi; Lydion, Phrygion, Dôrion; hoi de tous hepta tinas; Mixolydion, Lydion, Phrygion, Dôrion, Hypolydion, Hypophrygion, Hypodôrion, toutôn poios estin oxyteros? ho Mixolydios, k.t.l.** And Gaudentius (p. 21, l. 2) **kath' hekaston tropon hê tonon.** Cp. Dionys. Hal. *De Comp. Verb.* c. 19.

[7] *Anonymi scriptio de Musica* (Berlin. 1841).

[8] This is especially evident in the case of the Lichanos; as was observed by Aristides Quintilianus, who says (p. 10 Meib.): **hai kai tô genei lichanoi prosêgoreuthêsan, homônymôs tô plêttonti daktylô tên êchousan autas chordên onomastheisai.** But Tritê also is doubtless originally the 'third string' rather than the 'third note.'

[9] The correspondence between ancient and modern musical notation was first determined in a satisfactory way by Bellermann (*Die Tonleitern und Musiknoten der Griechen*), and Fortlage (*Das musicalische System der Griechen*).

[10] This observation was made by ancient writers, *e.g.* by Adrastus (Peripatetic philosopher of the second cent. A.D.): **epêuxêmenês de tês mousikês kai polychordôn kai polyphthongôn gegonotôn organôn tô proslêphthênai kai epi to bary kai epi to oxy tois pro[:y]parchousin oktô phthongois allous pleionas, homôs k.t.l.** (Theon Smyrn. c. 6).

[11] The epigram is quoted in the pseudo-Euclidean *Introductio*, p. 19 (Meib.): **ho de** (sc. **Iôn**) **en dekachordô lyra** (*i.e.* in a poem on the subject of the ten-stringed lyre):—

**tên dekabamona taxin echousa
tas symphônousas harmonias triodous;
prin men s' heptatonon psallon dia tessara pantes
Hellênes, spanian mousan aeiramenoi.**

'The triple ways of music that are in concord' must be the three conjunct tetrachords that can be formed with ten notes (*b c d e f g a bb c d*). This is the scale of the Lesser Perfect System before the addition of the Proslambanomenos.

[12] Pherecrates **cheirôn** fr. 1 (quoted by Plut. *de Mus.* c. 30). It is needless to refer to the other traditions on the subject, such as we find in Nicomachus (*Harm.* p. 35) and Boethius.

[13] The term **hyperypatê** had all but disappeared from the text of Theon Smyrnaeus in the edition of Bullialdus (Paris, 1644), having been corrupted into **hypatê** or **parypatê** in every place except one (p. 141, 3). It has been restored from MSS. in the edition of Hiller (Teubner, Leipzig, 1878). The word occurs also in Aristides Quintilianus (p. 10 Meib.), where the plural **hyperypatai** is used for the notes below Hypatê, and in Boethius (*Mus.* i. 20).

It may be worth noticing also that Thrasyllus uses the words **diezeugmenê** and **hyperbolaia** in the sense of **nêtê diezeugmenôn** and **nêtê hyperbolaiôn** (Theon Smyrn. *l. c.*).

[14] The *Introduction to Harmonics* (**eisagôgê harmonikê**) which bears the name of Euclid in modern editions (beginning with J. Pena, Paris, 1557) cannot be his work. In some MSS. it is ascribed to Cleonides, in others to Pappus, who was probably of the fourth century A. D. The author is one of the **harmonikoi** or Aristoxeneans, who adopt the method of equal temperament. He may perhaps be assigned to a comparatively early period on the ground that he recognises only the thirteen keys ascribed to Aristoxenus—not the fifteen keys given by most later writers (Aristides Quint., p. 22 Meib.). For some curious evidence connecting it with the name of the otherwise unknown writer Cleonides, see K. von Jan, *Die Harmonik des Aristoxenianers Kleonides* (Landsberg, 1870). The *Section of the Canon* (**kanonos katatomê**) belongs to the mathematical or Pythagorean school, dividing the tetrachord into two major tones and a **leimma** which is somewhat less than a semitone. In point of form it is decidedly Euclidean: but we do not find it referred to by any writer before the third century A. D.—the earliest testimony being that of Porphyry (pp. 272-276 in Wallis' edition).

[15] Plato, Rep. p. 399: **ouk ara, ên d' egô, polychordias ge oude panarmoniou hêmin deêsei en tais ôdais te kai melesin. Ou moi, ephê, phainetai. Trigônôn ara kai pêktidôn kai pantôn organôn hosa polychorda kai polyarmonia dêmiourgous ou threpsomen. Ou phainometha. Ti de? aulopoious ê aulêtas paradexei eis tên polin? ê ou touto polychordotaton, kai auta ta panarmonia aulou tynchanei onta mimêma? Dêla dê, ê d' hos. Lyra dê soi, ên d' egô, kai kithara leipetai, kai kata polin chrêsima; kai au kat' agrous tois nomeusi syrinx an tis eiê.**

The **aulos** was not exactly a flute. It had a mouthpiece which gave it the character rather of the modern oboe or clarinet: see the *Dictionary of Antiquities*, s. v. TIBIA. The **panarmonion** is not otherwise known, and the passage in Plato does not enable us to decide whether it was a real instrument or only a scale or arrangement of notes.

[16] The passage quoted above from the *Knights* of Aristophanes (p. 7) is sufficient to show that a marked preference for the Dorian mode would be a matter for jest.

[17] *Die Lehre von den Tonempfindungen*, p. 367, ed. 1863.

[18] So in the Euclidean *Sectio Canonis* the propositions which deal with the 'movable' notes, viz. Paranêtê and Lichanos (Theor. xvii) and Parhypatê and Tritê (Theor. xviii), begin by postulating the Mesê (**estô gar mesê ho B k.t.l.**).

[19] The term **hêgemôn** or 'leading note' of the tetrachord Mesôn, here applied to the Mesê, is found in the same sense in Plutarch, *De Mus.* c. 11, where **ho peri ton hêgemona keimenos tonos**] means the disjunctive tone. Similarly Ptolemy (*Harm.* i. 16) speaks of the tones in a diatonic scale as being **en tois hêgoumenois topois**, the semitones **en tois hepomenois** (sc. of the tetrachord): and again of the ratio 5:4 (the major Third) as the 'leading' one of an Enharmonic tetrachord (**ton epitetarton hos estin hêgoumenos tou enarmoniou genous**).

[20] The investigation occupies a considerable space in his *Harmonics*, viz. pp. 27-29 Meib. (from the words **peri de synecheias kai tou hexês**), and again pp. 58-72 Meib.

[21] This point is one which Aristoxenus is fond of insisting upon: cp. p. 10, 16 **ou pros tên katapyknôsin blepontas hôsper hoi harmonikoi**: p. 38, 3 **hoti de estin hê katapyknôsis ekmelês kai panta tropon achrêstos phaneron**: p. 53, 3 **kata tên tou melous physin zêteteon to hexês kai ouch hôs hoi eis tên katapyknôsin blepontes eiôthasin apodidonai to hexês**.

The statement that the ancient diagrams gave a series of twenty-eight successive dieses or quarter-tones has not been explained. The number of quarter-tones in an octave is only twenty-four. Possibly it is a mere error of transcription (κη for κδ). If not, we may perhaps connect it with the seven intervals of the ordinary octave scale, and the simple method by which the enharmonic intervals were expressed in the instrumental notation. It has been explained that raising a note a quarter of a tone was shown by turning it through a quarter of a circle. Thus, our *c* being denoted by **E** , *c*\* was **Ш** , and *c♯* was **Э** . Now the ancient diagrams, which divided every tone into four parts, must have had a character for *c♯*\*, or the note three-quarters of a tone above *c*. Naturally this would be the remaining position of **E** , namely **m** . Again, we have seen that when the interval between two notes on the diatonic scale is only a semitone, the result of the notation is to produce a certain number of duplicates, so to speak. Thus: **K** stands for *b*, and therefore **Х** for *c*: but *c* is a note of the original scale, and as such is written **П** . It may be that the diagrams to which Aristoxenus refers made use of these duplicates: that is to say, they may have made use of all four positions of a character (such as **K  ⊻  Х  ⊼** ) whether the interval to be filled was a tone or a semitone. If so, the seven intervals would give twenty-eight characters (besides the upper octave-note), and apparently therefore twenty-eight dieses. Some traces of this use of characters in four positions have been noticed by Bellermann (*Tonleitern*, p. 65).]

[22] The fullest account of this curious fragment of notation is that given by Bellermann in his admirable book, *Die Tonleitern und Musiknoten der Griechen*, pp. 61-65. His conjectures as to its origin do not claim a high degree of probability. See the remarks on pp. 97-99.

[23] Cp. Plato, *Rep.* p. 531: **kai smikrotaton einai touto diastêma, hô metrêteon.** It may even be that this sense of **harmonia** was connected with the use for the Enharmonic genus. It is at least worth notice that the phrase **ha ekaloun harmonias** in this passage answers to the adjective **enarmoniôn** in the passage first quoted (compare the words **peri autôn monon tôn hepta oktachordôn ha ekaloun harmonias** with **peri systêmatôn oktachordôn enarmoniôn monon**).

[24] So in Plato, *Leg.* p. 665 a: **tê dê tês kinêseôs taxei rhythmos onoma eiê, tê d' au tês phônês, tou te oxeos hama kai bareos synkerannymenôn, harmonia onoma prosagoreuoito.**

[25] Ptol. *Harm.* ii. 6. After drawing a distinction between difference of key as affecting the whole of a melody or piece of music and as a means of change in the course of it—the distinction, in short, between transposition and modulation proper—he says of the latter: **hautê de hôsper ekpiptein autên** (sc. **tên aisthêsin**) **poiei tou synêthous kai prosdokômenou melous, hotan epi pleon men syneirêtai to akolouthon, metabainê de pê pros heteron eidos, êtoi kata to genos ê kata tên tasin.** That is to say, the sense of change is produced by a change of genus or of pitch. A change of *species* is not suggested. So Dionys. Hal. *De Comp. Verb.* c. 19 **hoi de ge dithyrambopoioi kai tous tropous** (keys) **meteballon, Dôrikous te kai Phrygious kai Lydious en tô autô asmati poiountes; kai tas melôdias exêllatton, tote men enarmonious poiountes, k.t.l.**

[26] Since this was written I have learned from Mr. H. S. Jones that the form **E** for beta occurs on an inscription dated about 500 B.C., viz. Count Tyszkiewicz's bronze plate, published simultaneously by Robert in the *Monumenti Antichi pubblicati per cura della reale Accademia dei Lincei*, i. pp. 593 (with plate), and Fröhner in the *Revue Archéologique*, 1891 July-August, pp. 51 ff. Pl. xix. Mr. Jones points out that this **E** connects the crescent beta ( **C** ) of Naxos, Delos, &c. with the common form, and is evidently therefore an early form of the letter.

I take this opportunity of thanking Mr. Jones for other help, especially in regard to the subject of this section.

[27] *Harmonik und Melopöie*, p. 286 (ed. 1863). The true form of the letter is given by Mr. Roberts, *Greek Epigraphy*, p. 109.

[28] Pausanias (iv. 27, 4) says of the founding of Messene: **eirgazonto de kai hypo mousuiês allês men oudemias, aulôn de Boiôtiôn kai Argeiôn; ta te Sakada kai Pronomou melê tote dê proêchthê malista eis hamillan.**

[29] *Harm.* ii. 8 **hoi de hyperekpiptontes tou dia pasôn tous ap' autou tou dia pasôn apôterô parelkontôs hypotithentai, tous autous aei ginomenous tois proeilêmmenois.**

[30] *Harm.* ii. 11 **hôste mêd' an heteron eti doxai tô eidei ton tonon para ton proteron, all' hypodôrion palin, ê ton auton hypophrygion, oxyphônoteron tinos ê baryphônoteron monon.**

[31] *Harm.* ii. 7 **pros tên toiautên diaphoran hê tôn organôn holôn epitasis ê palin anesis aparkei.**

[32] This may be traced in the occasionally controversial tone; as *Harm.* ii. 7 **hoi men ep' elatton tou dia pasôn phthasantes, hoi d' ep' auto monon, hoi de epi to meizon toutou, prokopên tina schedon toiautên aei tôn neôterôn para tous palaioterous thêrômenôn, anoikeion tês peri to hêrmosmenon physeôs te kai apokatastaseôs; hê monê perainein anankaion esti tên tôn esomenôn akrôn tonôn diastasin.** We may compare c. 11.

[33] So Bacch. p. 19 Meib. **theseis de tetrachordôn hois to melos horizetai eisin hepta? synaphê, diazeuxis, hypodiazeuxis, k.t.l.** (see the whole passage).

[34] We may think of this as a scale in which the semitones are considerably smaller, *i.e.* in which *c* and *f* are nearly a quarter of a tone flat.

[35] Ptol. *Harm.* ii. 16 **periechetai de ta men en tê lyra kaloumena sterea tonou tinos hypo tôn tou toniaiou diatonou arithmôn tou autou tonou, ta de malaka hypo tôn en tô migmati tou malakou chrômatos apithmôn tou autou tonou.** Here **tonou tinos** evidently means 'of any given key,' and **tou autou tonou** 'of that key.' There is either no restriction, or none that Ptolemy thought worth mentioning, in the choice of the key and species.

[36] The two passages enumerate the scales in a slightly different manner. In i. 16 they are arranged in view of the genus or colour into—

Pure Middle Soft Diatonic, viz.—
**sterea**, of the lyre.

**tritai**      } of the cithara.
**hypertropa** }


Mixture of Chromatic, viz.—
**malaka**, of the lyre.
**tropika**, of the cithara.


Mixture of Soft Diatonic, viz.—
**parypatai**, of the cithara.


Mixture of **diatonon syntonon**, viz.—
**lydia** } of the cithara.
**iastia** }

It is added, however, that in their use of this last 'mixture' musicians are in the habit of tuning the cithara in the Pythagorean manner, with two Major tones and a **leimma** (called **diatonon ditoniaion**).

In the second passage (ii. 16) the scales of the lyre are given first, then those of the cithara with the key of each. The order is the same, except that **parypatai** comes before **tropika** (now called **tropoi**), and **lydia** is placed last. The words **ta de lydia hoi tou toniaiou diatonou** [sc. **arithmoi periechousi tou dôriou** cannot be correct, not merely because they contradict the statement of the earlier passage that **lydia** denoted a mixture with **diatonon syntonon** (or in practice **diatonon ditoniaion**), but also because the scales that do not admit mixture are placed first in the list in both passages. Hence we should doubtless read **ta de lydia hoi [tou migmatos] tou [di]toniaiou diatonou tou Dôriou**.]

[37] *Harm.* i. 16 **plên kathoson adousi men akolouthôs tô dedeigmenô syntonô diatonikô, kathaper exestai skopein apo tês tôn oikeiôn autou logôn parabolês, harmozontai de heteron ti genos** (sc. the Pythagorean), **xynengizon men ekeinô, k.t.l.**

[38] It seems needless to set out these melodies here. The first satisfactory edition of them is that of Bellermann, *Die Hymnen des Dionysius und Mesomedes* (Berlin, 1840). They are given by Westphal in his *Musik des griechischen Alterthumes* (1883), and by Gevaert, *Musique de l'Antiquité*, vol. i. pp. 445 ff.; also in Mr. W. Chappell's *History of Music* (London, 1874), where the melodies

of the first and third hymns will be found harmonised by the late Sir George Macfarren.

The melody published by Kircher (*Musurgia*, i. p. 541) as a fragment of the first Pythian ode of Pindar has no attestation, and is generally regarded as a forgery.

[39] Of the discovery made at Delphi, after most of this book was in type, I hope to say something in the *Appendix*.

[40] *Harm.* p. 18 Meib. **legetai gar dê kai logôdes ti melos, to synkeimenon ek tôn prosôdiôn, to en tois onomasi; physikon gar to epiteinein kai anienai en tô dialegesthai.**

[41] I need not repeat what is said by Dr. Wessely and M. Ruelle in defence of the genuineness of our fragment. They justly point to the remarkable coincidence that the music of this very play is quoted by Dionysius of Halicarnassus (*l. c.*). It would almost seem as if it was the only well-known specimen of music of the classical period of tragedy.

The transcription of Dr. Crusius, with his conjectural restorations, will be found in the *Appendix*. I have only introduced one of his corrections here, viz. the note on the second syllable of **kateklysen.**

[42] Dr. Crusius, however, detects a Φ; (the sign for *g*) over the first syllable of **kateklusen** and the second syllable of **pontou**. There is little trace of them in his facsimile.

[43] This argument is used, along with some others not so cogent, in Mr. W. Chappell's *History of Music* (p. 130).

[44] Ps. Eucl. *Introd.* p. 20 Meib. **kata systêma de hotan ek synaphês eis diazeuxin ê anapalin metabolê ginêtai.** Anonym. § 65 **systêmatikai de (sc. metabolai) hopotan ek diazeuxeôs eis synaphên ê empalin metelthê to melos.**

[45] As represented primarily by the analysis of Helmholtz, *Die Tonempfindungen*, p. 467, ed. 1863.

[46] *Harmonik und Melopöie*, p. 356 (ed. 1863): 'Die älteste griechische Tonart ist demnach eine Molltonart.... Aus Kleinasien wurden zunächst zwei Durtonarten nach Griechenland eingeführt, die lydische und phrygische.' In the 1886 edition of the same book (p. 189) Westphal discovers a similar classification of modes implied in the words of Plato, *Rep.* p. 400 a **tri' atta estin eidê ex hôn hai baseis plekontai, hôsper en tois phthongois tettara hothen hai pasai harmoniai.** But Plato is evidently referring to some matter of common knowledge. The three forms or elements of which all rhythms are made up are of course the ratios 1: 1, 2: 1 and 3: 2, which

yield the three kinds of rhythm, dactylic, iambic and cretic (answering to common, triple, and quintuple time). Surely the four elements of all musical scales of which Plato speaks are not four kinds of scale (*Harmonien-Klassen*), but the four ratios which give the primary musical intervals—viz. the ratios 2: 1, 3: 2, 4: 3 and 9: 8, which give the Octave, Fifth, Fourth and Tone.

[47] If Hypo-phrygian is the same as the older Ionian (p. 11), the coincidence is complete for the time of Aristotle. Plato treats the claim of Ionian to rank among the Hellenic modes as somewhat doubtful (*Laches*, p. 188).

[48] Aristox. *Harm.* p. 23 Meib. **hoi men gar tê nun katechousê melopoiia ounêtheis monon ontes eiktôs tên ditonon lichanon** (*f* in the scale *e-a*) **exorizousi; suntonôterais gar chrôntai schedon hoi pleistoi tôn nun. toutou d' aition to boulesthai glukainein aei. sêmeion de hoti toutou stochazontai, malista men gar kai pleiston chronon en tô chrômati diatribousin. hotan d' aphikôntai pote eis tên harmonian engus tou chromatos prosagousi, sunepismômenou tou êthous.**

[49] Ibid. p. 26 **noêteon gar apeirous ton arithmon tas lichanous. hou gar an stêsês tên phônên apodedeigmenon lichanô topou lichanos estai; diakenon de ouden esti tou lichanoeidous topou, oude toiouton hôste mê dechisthai lichanon.** And p. 48 **epeidê per ho tês lichanou topos eis apeirous temnetai tomas.**

[50] Aristox. *Harm.* p. 69 Meib. **kata men oun ta megethê tôn diastêmatôn kai tas tôn phthongôn taseis apeira pôs phainetai einai ta peri to melos, kata de tas dynameis kai kata ta eidê kai kata tas theseis peperasmena te kai tetagmena.**

[51] The ecclesiastical Modes received their final shape in the *Dodecachordon* of Glareanus (Bâle, 1547). They are substantially the Greek modes of Westphal's theory, although the Greek names which Glareanus adopted seem to have been chosen at haphazard. But the ecclesiastical Modes, as Helmholtz points out, were developed under the influence of polyphonic music from the earlier stages represented by the Ambrosian and Gregorian scales. It would be a singular chance if they were also, as Greek modes, the source from which the Ambrosian and Gregorian scales were themselves derived.

Some further hints on this part of the subject may possibly be derived from the musical scales in use among nations that have not attained to any form of harmony, such as the Arabians, the Indians, or the Chinese. A valuable collection of these scales is given by Mr. A. J. Ellis at the end of his translation of Helmholtz (Appendix XX. Sect. K, *Non-harmonic Scales*). Among the most interesting for our purpose are the eight mediaeval Arabian scales given on the authority of Professor Land (nos. 54-61). The first three of these—called 'Ochaq, Nawa and Boasili—follow the Pythagorean intonation, and answer respectively to the Hypo-phrygian, Phrygian, and Mixo-lydian species of the octave. The next two—Rast and Zenkouleh—are also Hypo-phrygian in species, but the Third and Sixth are flatter by about an eighth of a tone (the Pythagorean comma). In Zenkouleh the Fifth also is similarly flattened. The last two scales—Hhosaini and Hhidjazi—are Phrygian: but the Second and Fifth, and in the case of Hhidjazi also the Sixth, are flatter by the interval of a comma. The remaining scale, called Rahawi, does not fall under any species, since the semitones are between the Third and Fourth, and again between the Fifth and Sixth. It will be seen that in general character—though by no means in details—this series of scales bears a considerable resemblance to the 'scales of the cithara' as given by Ptolemy (*supra*, p. 85). In both cases the several scales are distinguished from each other partly by the order of the intervals (*species*), partly by the intonation, or magnitude of the intervals employed (*genus*). This latter element is conspicuously absent from the ecclesiastical Modes.

[52] *Tonempfindungen*, p. 364 (ed. 1863).

[53] Aristox., *Harm.* p. 3 Meib. **kineitai men gar kai dialegomenôn hêmôn kai melôdountôn tên eirêmenên kinêsin; oxy gar kai bary dêlon hôs en amphoterois toutois enestin.** Also p. 8 **dyo tines eisin ideai kinêseôs, hê te synechês kai hê diastêmatikê; kata men oun tên synechê topon tina diexienai phainetai hê phônê tê aisthêsei houtôs hôs an mêdamou histamenê, k.t.l.** And p. 9 **tên oun synechê logikên einai phanen, k.t.l.**

[54] Ibid. p. 18 Meib. **tou ge logôdous kechôristai tautê to mousikon melos; legetai gar dê kai logôdes ti melos, to synkeimenon ek tôn prosôdiôn tôn en tois onomasin; physikon gar to epiteinein kai anienai en tô dialegesthai.**

[55] Nicomachus, *Enchiridion*, p. 4 **ei gar tis ê dialegomenos ê apologoumenos tini ê anaginôskôn ge ekdêla metaxy kath' hekaston phthongon poiei ta megethê, diistanôn kai metaballôn tên phônên ap' allou eis allon, ouketi legein ho toioutos oude anaginôskein alla meleazein legetai.**

[56] *De Compositione Verborum*, c. 11, p. 58 Reisk.

[57] *De Comp.* c. 11, p. 64 **to de auto ginetai kai peri tous rhythmous; hê men gar pezê lexis oudenos oute onomatos oute rhêmatos biazetai tous chronous oude metatithêsin, all' oias pareilêphe tê physei tas syllabas, tas te makras kai tas bracheias, toiautas phylattei; hê de mousikê te kai rhythmikê metaballousin autas meiousai kai parauxousai, ôite pollakis eis tanantia metachôrein; ou gar tais syllabais apeuthynousi tous chronous, alla tois chronois tas syllabas.**

[58] The metrical accent or ictus was marked in ancient notation by points placed over the accented syllable. These points have been preserved in Mr. Ramsay's musical inscription (see the Appendix, p. 133) and in one or two places of the fragment of the *Orestes* (p. 130). Hence Dr. Crusius has been able to restore the rhythm with tolerable certainty, and has made the interesting discovery that in both pieces the ictus falls as a rule on a short syllable. The only exceptions in the inscription are circumflexed syllables, where the long vowel or diphthong is set to two notes, the first of which is short and accented. The accents on the short first syllables of the dochmiacs of Euripides are a still more unexpected evidence of the same rhythmical tendency.

[59] Plato, *Legg.* p. 669.

[60] On this point I may refer to the somewhat fuller treatment in Smith's *Dictionary of Antiquities*, art. MUSICA (Vol. II, p. 199, ed. 1890-91).

[61] Plato, *Legg.* p. 812 d **panta oun ta toiauta mê prospherein tois mellousin en trisin etesi to tês mousikês chrêsimon eklêpsesthai dia tachous.**

[62] In Euclid's *Sectio Canonis* the Pythagorean division is assumed, and there is no hint of any other ratio than those which Pythagoras discovered. Prop. xvii shows how to find the Enharmonic Lichanos and Paranêtê by means of the Fourth and Fifth. Prop. xviii proves against Aristoxenus (of course without naming him), that a **pyknon** cannot be divided into two equal intervals; but there is no attempt to explain the nature of the Enharmonic diesis. It is worth notice that in these propositions the Lichanos and Paranêtê of the Enharmonic scale are called **lichanos** and **paranêtê** simply, as though the Enharmonic were the only genus—a usage which agrees with that of the Aristotelian *Problems* (supra, p. 33).

According to Ptolemy (i. 13) the Pythagorean philosopher Archytas was the author of a new division of the tetrachord for each of the three genera. In it the natural Major Third (5: 4) was given for the large interval of the Enharmonic, in place of the Pythagorean ditone (81: 64); and the Diatonic was the same as the Middle Soft Diatonic of Ptolemy. But, as Westphal long ago pointed out (*Harmonik und Melopöie*, p. 230, ed. 1863), this scheme is probably the work of the later Pythagorean school. It seems to be unknown to Plato and Aristoxenus,—the latter wrote a life of Archytas—and also to Euclid, as we have seen. The next scheme of musical ratios is that of Eratosthenes, who makes no use of the natural Major Third.

[63] The two schools distinguished by Plato seem to be those which were afterwards known as the **harmonikoi** or Aristoxeneans, and the **mathêmatikoi**, who carried on the tradition of Pythagoras. The

**harmonikoi** regarded a musical interval as a quantity which could be measured directly by the ear, without reference to the numerical ratio upon which it might be based. They practically adopted the system of equal temperament. The **mathêmatikoi** sought for ratios, but by experiment 'among the consonances which are heard,' as Plato says. Hence they failed equally with those whose method never rose above the facts of sense.

# Booksophile
### Your Local Online Bookstore

Buy Books Online from
# www.Booksophile.com

Explore our collection of books written in various languages and uncommon topics from different parts of the world, including history, art and culture, poems, autobiography and bibliographies, cooking, action & adventure, world war, fiction, science, and law.

Add to your bookshelf or gift to another lover of books - first editions of some of the most celebrated books ever published. From classic literature to bestsellers, you will find many first editions that were presumed to be out-of-print.

Free shipping globally for orders worth US$ 100.00.

Use code "Shop_10" to avail additional 10% on first order.

Visit today
*www.booksophile.com*

Printed by BoD™in Norderstedt, Germany

9 789357 913621